THE CURRY SECRET

Indian Restaurant Cookery At Home

Kris Dhillon

RIGHT WAY

CONTENTS

INTRODUCTION

Many difficulties stand in the way of anyone trying to explore the secrets of Indian Restaurant cooking. People buy an Indian Cook book but find that traditional recipes and methods can be disappointing when they produce a home cooked taste and not the distinct flavour of Restaurant curries. This is not really surprising as the art of Restaurant cooking is a very closely kept secret, next to impossible to uncover.

A Top Chef guards these Trade Secrets closely, knowing that he may become dispensable should the proprietor acquire his skills. A proprietor who is also the Chef aims to satisfy his customers, but also keeps this knowledge close to his heart.

At the risk of upsetting my contemporaries, I have chosen to reveal all. The following pages will show you simply and precisely how to create the curries you love, in your own kitchen, using the same techniques as your favourite Restaurants. Secret recipes, special little "tricks of the trade", have all been included to give you the knowledge to reproduce that special taste that, until now, may well have eluded you.

WEIGHTS AND MEASURES

Both metric and imperial measurements have been given in this book with the metric measures being rounded up or down to the nearest unit. Remember to use one or the other and not to combine imperial and metric measurements in one recipe.

All spoon measurements throughout the book are slightly rounded spoonfuls unless specified as being level.

One cupful equals one teacup size which is approximately a quarter pint or 5 fluid ounces. The important thing is to use the same cup throughout one recipe.

1

Spices and Herbs

The curries in this book require quantities of the following spices and herbs, so it is essential to get these together and to prepare them as suggested before you begin cooking. I think it is safe to say that most supermarkets and grocers now stock these items with perhaps the exception of the black cardamoms. Ethnic grocers will certainly have supplies of both fresh and dry ingredients available all year round.

Other than for rice dishes, Restaurants do not generally use spices in their whole form. However, they will buy them whole and then grind small quantities at a time for the best flavour. I suggest in general that you follow this example. An electric coffee-grinder is ideal for the grinding as it grinds the spices to the fineness required for Restaurant curries. (Alternatively you could use a pestle and mortar.) This degree of fineness is not of particular importance for home cooking, but a Restaurant Chef is meticulous in this requirement and will test the ground spices between forefinger and thumb, being satisfied only when the mixture feels perfectly smooth. This is quite a task with the amounts needed for a busy Restaurant, but easy enough when grinding a few tablespoons at home.

When storing the dry ingredients, use glass or plastic containers with well fitting lids and keep in a cool, dry place away from strong light. Whole spices will keep their flavour for months when stored in this way. Remember to label all your containers clearly as it is extremely difficult to tell which spice is which after they have been ground.

For those of you who are new to Indian cooking, the following descriptions should be helpful when buying the spices and herbs you will need.

AMBCHOOR – This is a powder made from dried green mangoes and has a unique sweet and sour taste. Buy small quantities as you will require relatively little of this ingredient.

BAYLEAVES – These will be familiar to cooks as they are used for flavouring all sorts of dishes of many different origins. In Indian cooking we use them whole for rice dishes and grind them with other ingredients to make *garam masala*.

CARDAMOMS (*green*) – Small, whitish green pods full of dark, sweetly aromatic seeds. Used in sweet and savoury dishes.

CARDAMOMS (*black*) – Larger than their green counterparts, these are dark brown in colour with a stronger flavour and aroma. They are an important ingredient in *garam masala*.

CHILLIES (*green*) – These vary in length from about 1 inch (2.5cm) to over 4 inches (10cm), have a dark green flesh and flat, round white seeds. Generally speaking the small chillies have a tendency to be hotter than the larger ones so will work out more economical. Besides providing the heat in Indian foods, green chillies impart a special flavour not found with the dried red chillies.

Store whole and unwashed in paper, and place in the salad compartment of a refrigerator.

Freezing: Grind in a blender or food processor with a little water and freeze in ice-cube trays. Fresh green chillies are past their best after a week or two so this is a good idea if you cook Indian food infrequently.

NB. Handle cut chillies very carefully as the irritant in them will cause a burning sensation on contact with skin. Always wash your hands before touching your face.

CHILLIES (*red powder*) – Chilli powder adds colour to Indian curries as well as heat and flavour. Unlike other dry ingredients which are best bought whole, I recommend that you buy these ready ground as chilli powder. The reason for this is that grinding red chillies requires particular care as the fine powder will escape to irritate eyes, nose and throat causing terrible bouts of sneezing and runny eyes.

CINNAMON – Buy sticks, as pieces of cinnamon are used in rice dishes. It is ground with other spices in *garam masala*.

CLOVES – These are used for their flavour and aroma, whole in rice dishes and ground for *garam masala*.

CORIANDER (*fresh green*) – This is easily the most wonderful, versatile and widely used herb of all in Indian cooking, both in the home and the Restaurant. Commercially grown coriander is taller – growing to some 10 inches (25cm) or so – than the home grown variety and is readily available from ethnic grocers and greengrocers. The flavour and aroma of this lovely herb makes it a vital ingredient for turning a good Indian dish into an excellent one, whether stirred into a curry or sprinkled onto hot food as a garnish.

Use leaves and stems and chop finely (discarding any tough pieces) and add to food right at the end of cooking as the delicate flavour is easily lost.

Fresh coriander will keep well for a week or so if you immerse the stems in a container of water rather as you would a bunch of flowers.

CORIANDER SEEDS – As delicate in flavour as the plant from which they come, these seeds are small, round and beige in colour. In the Restaurant, coriander is ground and used as a spice in its own right as well as in *garam masala*.

CUMMIN SEEDS – These look like caraway seeds, have quite a strong flavour and are used in Restaurant cooking mostly in their ground form.

CUMMIN SEEDS (*black*) – Finer and darker than regular cummin this spice is also more expensive. It is unlikely that you will find black cummin in supermarkets so you may have to go to an Indian or Pakistani grocer. If you cannot get it, you may use regular cummin as a substitute.

FENUGREEK (*dry leaves*) – Not to be confused with fenugreek seeds, this is a dark green leafy plant similar in height to coriander. The flavour is not as subtle as that of coriander and becomes more concentrated when the plant is dried. Known as 'Methi' it is available from Asian grocers in both its fresh and dry form. It is the dry ingredient that is used in Restaurant cooking and although fenugreek is perhaps not an essential herb for Restaurant curries, it certainly adds that 'extra something' so is worth trying if you can get it.

To prepare for use, pick out and discard any straw-like pieces. Grind in a coffee-grinder, sieve and store in a glass jar. Do not forget to label.

GARLIC – A familiar and popular herb, garlic is particularly necessary for the flavour of Restaurant curries where it is used in generous amounts. Buy bulbs that have firm, plump cloves and store in a cool dry place as you would onions.

GINGER (*fresh*) – This looks like a thick, knobbly root. Scraping away the pale brown skin reveals a creamy yellow, slightly fibrous interior. The fresher the ginger the less fibrous it tends to be, so to ensure freshness, look for plump pieces with a taut skin.

To store, keep in a cool dry airy place as you would other vegetables.

Freezing: Peel and grind into a paste with a little water and freeze in ice-cube trays. You can then take out a cube or two as you require it.

NUTMEG – Nutmegs can be bought from supermarkets as well as Indian grocers. Buy whole, and break into pieces by hitting lightly with a hammer or rolling pin before grinding.

PAPRIKA – A personal favourite, paprika is excellent for adding colour and a very slightly tangy/sweet flavour to curries. It can be bought in small tins with tight fitting plastic lids which is an ideal way of storing this spice. If buying in polythene bags transfer to a glass jar and label, as it is difficult to distinguish between paprika and chilli powder without tasting.

TURMERIC – This spice is used in Indian cooking mainly for its yellow colour although it also aids the digestion and has a mild, earthy flavour. Buy turmeric that is a bright yellow colour and handle carefully as it will stain the hands and clothes.

GARAM MASALA

The *garam* means hot and the masala a *mixture of spices*, so this is a *hot spice mixture*. The heat however is not a heat that you taste as with chillies, but one that affects the body. This theory originates from the Hindu concept of medicine and diet called *tridosha*, which teaches that some foods have a warming effect on the body while others have a cooling one. Spices such as cloves, cinnamon, black cardamoms and nutmeg are the *garam* constituents of this aromatic mixture.

The garam masala should be put into foods towards the end of cooking and is sometimes also sprinkled onto cooked meat, vegetables and yoghurts as a garnish.

HOW TO MAKE GARAM MASALA

This makes about 3 tablespoons.

1 tablespoon coriander seeds
1 tablespoon cummin
1 teaspoon green cardamoms
1 teaspoon cloves
1 teaspoon black peppercorns

Garam Masala ingredients (contd.)
2 sticks cinnamon approx. 2 inches (5cm) in length
2 bayleaves
½ a small nutmeg
4 black cardamoms

Place all ingredients in an electric coffee-grinder and grind for 1 minute. Carefully remove lid and test by rubbing a little of the mixture between forefinger and thumb. Finely ground spices should not feel gritty. If necessary switch on machine for another few seconds.

Put the garam masala into a small airtight container, preferably made of glass or plastic, and label.

There are various other mixtures and condiments used in this book which I feel may require explanation:

CHAT MASALA – This is a ready mixed preparation of salt and spices used for the "chats". It is available from Asian and Pakistani grocers in small boxes.

FOOD COLOURINGS – These are used quite widely in Restaurant cooking. Buy the powdered rather than liquid variety for greater potency.

VEGETABLE GHEE – This is used mainly for making the rice dishes and the only other suitable alternative is the ghee made from clarifying butter. Something I have found particularly good if you do not wish to do this, and cannot get vegetable ghee, is concentrated butter. This is readily available from supermarkets and shops.

2

Snacks and Nibbles

Indian Restaurants do not serve snacks as such but rather what may be termed little nibbles that are eaten with a drink while waiting for your meal. These tasty morsels are however very popular, so I have included them as I feel no book on Restaurant cookery would be complete without them.

I have, as promised, included the "tricks of the trade" required to produce the appearance and flavour typical of Indian food.

POPADOMS

The Restaurant method of cooking popadoms will produce far better results than the usual method of simply frying which can leave the popadoms rather greasy.

Please read the instructions carefully and have all utensils ready before you begin.

Plain and/or spicy popadoms
Vegetable oil for deep frying

Heat the oil in a large deep frying pan until very hot but not smoking.

Take TWO popadoms at a time, and holding them as one, carefully slip them into the hot oil. As soon as they are immersed turn them over using tongs or two fish slices. Hold the two popadoms together as one all the time. Allow no more than two seconds and remove popadoms from the hot oil.

Drain on kitchen paper upright (like toast in a toast rack), and not flat, for the best results.

Note: In the Restaurant we use a large, aluminium colander for this purpose and put the fried popadoms in side by side. The colander is then placed in a "hot-plate", a piece of equipment rather like the bottom section of a "hostess" trolley. This technique allows the oil to drain away efficiently and keeps the popadoms warm, dry and crisp. Placing the cooked popadoms in a warm oven will of course be just as effective.

Popadoms may be cooked several hours in advance and warmed just before serving.

ONION SALAD

Served with popadoms together with the yoghurt mint sauce.

Preparation time: 5 minutes

2 cooking onions
1 tomato
½ inch (1cm) piece cucumber
generous pinch salt
pinch red chilli powder
1 teaspoon lemon juice
2 teaspoons mint sauce (the sort served with roast lamb)

Finely chop onions, tomato and cucumber to produce thin strips. Place in a bowl and add remaining ingredients. Mix thoroughly.

YOGHURT MINT SAUCE

Served with popadoms and a variety of starters.

Preparation time: 5 minutes

1 cup plain yoghurt
2 teaspoons mint sauce
½ level teaspoon salt
¼ teaspoon chilli powder
¼ teaspoon garam masala

Yoghurt Mint Sauce ingredients (contd.)
¼ teaspoon ambchoor
½ level teaspoon caster (or granulated) sugar
2 drops green food colouring (optional)

Put all ingredients into a bowl and mix well.

BOMBAY MIX

This is a mixture of nuts, besan sticks and spices served to customers in bowls to enjoy with their apperitifs. It is somewhat time consuming and fiddly to make, and to my knowledge Restaurants do not make it themselves. As most bought varieties are excellent I feel it is unnecessary to go to the time and trouble of making it yourself. Bombay mix is readily available from delicatessens, health food stores, shops, supermarkets as well as Asian grocers.

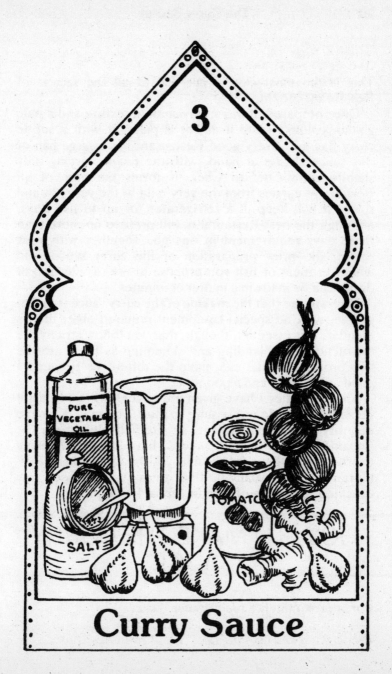

Curry Sauce

This is the most closely guarded of all the secrets of Restaurant cooking.

Once prepared, it has a very smooth texture and a pale golden colour. Taste it and it is pleasant with a subtle curry flavour. Every good Restaurant has a large pan of this sauce always at hand, with the recipe varying only slightly from Chef to Chef. It forms the base of all Restaurant curries from the very mild to the very hot and spicy. It will keep in a refrigerator for up to five days, although the best Restaurants will prepare no more than three days requirement in one go. Together with your spices, the prior preparation of the curry sauce, and whatever meat or fish you propose to use, a selection of dishes can be made in a matter of minutes.

You will see that the making of the curry sauce is in fact simple, with no special equipment required other than a blender. It is essential, though, that you follow strictly the instructions for blending and skimming as these are the two procedures that can make the difference between a good curry sauce and a poor one.

The quantities I have given are enough for six to eight persons. If you do not require so much you may halve the quantity of each ingredient, or alternatively, freeze the remainder of the finished sauce. I have included freezing instructions where applicable. Although Indian Restaurants do not usually do this, it is a perfectly good way of taking advantage of your freezer at home.

HOW TO MAKE THE CURRY SAUCE

For approximately 8 main course dishes

Preparation and cooking time: 1 hr 30 minutes approx.

2 lb (900g) cooking onions
2 oz (50g) green ginger
2 oz (50g) garlic
2¾ pint (1 litre 570ml) water
1 teaspoon salt
1 tin (8 oz/225g) tomatoes
8 tablespoons vegetable oil
1 teaspoon tomato purée
1 teaspoon turmeric
1 teaspoon paprika

STAGE 1.

Peel and rinse the onions, ginger and garlic. Slice the onions and roughly chop the ginger and garlic.

Put the chopped ginger and garlic into a blender with about ½ a pint (275ml) of the water and blend until smooth.

Take a large saucepan and put into it the onions, the blended garlic and ginger, and the remainder of the water.

Add the salt and bring to the boil. Turn down the heat to very low and simmer, with the lid on, for 40–45 minutes.

Leave to cool.

STAGE 2.

Once cooled, pour about half of the boiled onion mixture into a blender and blend until perfectly smooth. Absolute smoothness is essential. To be certain, blend for at least 2 minutes. Pour the blended onion mixture into a clean pan or bowl and repeat with the other half of the boiled onions.

Wash and dry the saucepan. Reserve about 4 tablespoons of the sauce at this stage to use in cooking the chicken (page 49) and lamb (page 63).

Freezing: Freezing is best done at this stage.

STAGE 3.

Open the can of tomatoes, pour into the rinsed blender jug, and blend. Again it is important that they are perfectly smooth so blend for about 2 minutes.

Into the clean saucepan, put the oil, tomato purée, turmeric and paprika.

Add the blended tomatoes and bring to the boil. Turn down the heat and cook, stirring occasionally, for 10 minutes.

Now add the onion mixture to the saucepan and bring to the boil again. Turn down the heat enough to keep the sauce at a simmer.

You will notice at this stage that a froth rises to the surface of the sauce. This needs to be skimmed off.

Keep simmering and skimming for 20-25 minutes, stirring now and again to prevent the sauce sticking to the bottom of the saucepan.

Use immediately or cool and refrigerate for up to 4 days.

4

Starters

MENU

TANDOORI CHICKEN – Spring chicken marinated in yoghurt, herbs and spices, cooked at high heat.

SEEKH KEBABS – Minced lamb with onions, herbs and spices.

LAMB TIKKA – Marinated lamb pieces cooked quickly at high heat.

CHICKEN TIKKA – Boneless diced chicken marinated and cooked quickly at high heat.

TANDOORI FISH – Succulent pieces of fish, marinated and grilled.

TANDOORI KING PRAWNS – Delicately spiced and cooked under a hot grill.

CHICKEN CHAT – Diced spring chicken in a spicy dressing, served on a crisp green salad.

ALOO CHAT – diced cooked potatoes, in a spicy dressing, served on a crisp green salad.

ONION BHAJEE – Besan (gram flour) flavoured with sliced onion, herbs and spices, deep fried until crisp on the outside and succulent on the inside.

TANDOOR COOKING

At one time it was believed that dishes cooked in a tandoor could not be satisfactorily reproduced at home using an ordinary convection oven. Whilst it may be true that cooking food on charcoal does give it a unique quality, I believe the very high temperatures that are reached in a tandoori oven are more significant than the charcoal that fires it. It is possible to achieve similar conditions at home by heating your oven to the highest possible temperature and cooking the food near the top of the oven where it will be at its hottest.

If you should wish to serve your starters in the same manner as served in Indian Restaurants, I have given instructions for sizzling them. A wonderful innovation which gives food a special tantalizing allure, it involves buying sizzler dishes. These are heavy, oval, cast iron plates readily available from department stores and suppliers of catering equipment.

HOW TO SIZZLE

Heat sizzler dish on the hob for about 5 minutes to get really hot.

Turn off the heat and place some sliced onion onto dish.

Immediately put cooked starter on top of the onion and pour 1 tablespoon of melted vegetable ghee onto side of dish. The heat from the dish rapidly heats the fat which, in contact with the onion, starts the sizzling.

Now squirt some lemon juice onto onions. This produces even more sizzling and a delicious aroma.

Finally, sprinkle with chopped coriander, and serve.

TANDOORI MARINADE

A variety of dishes require that the meat, fish or poultry is marinated prior to cooking. Follow this recipe wherever this is necessary.

Preparation time: 5 minutes

Makes two cups

Tandoori Marinade ingredients
2 cups plain yoghurt
2 green chillies
2 teaspoons grated green ginger
3 cloves garlic
1½ teaspoons salt
1 teaspoon red chilli powder
1 teaspoon black cummin
1½ teaspoons garam masala
2 teaspoons vinegar
2 tablespoons cooking oil
½ teaspoon red food colouring
½ teaspoon yellow food colouring

Combine the yoghurt, green chillies, ginger and garlic in a blender until smooth.

Empty into a bowl and add all the remaining ingredients. Beat the mixture until glossy.

TANDOORI CHICKEN

The secret is to buy a chicken of weight no more than 3 lb (1kg 250g). If you buy portions, ensure that these are from small chickens.

For a main course double the quantities of everything (including the marinade).

Preparation and cooking time: 25 minutes

Serves 4 (starters)

1 whole chicken or 4 portions
2 cups tandoori marinade

Quarter chicken if using a whole one, and remove the skin. Make deep slits into the meat right down to the bone, four into each leg portion and two into each breast portion. Wash, and drain well or wipe off excess moisture with kitchen paper.

Now put the chicken into the bowl containing the marinade and mix thoroughly making sure that the marinade goes into the slits.

Cover and refrigerate for at least 6 hours but preferably overnight. The chicken may be kept in the marinade for up to 3 days without spoiling.

Preheat oven to maximum temperature.

Shake off excess marinade from chicken portions and place on a rack in a shallow baking tray. Bake near top of oven for about 20 minutes. Test with a fork to make sure chicken is cooked, when the flesh will come away from the bone easily.

Serve immediately, sizzling if preferred, with a green salad, lemon wedges and yoghurt mint sauce (recipe page 17).

SEEKH KEBABS

These are made from lean minced lamb that is put through the mincer twice. The meat must be lean to give the correct flavour and texture. Mincing twice enhances the binding together of the meat.

Preparation and cooking time: 30 minutes

Serves 4

1 egg
1 tablespoon chopped onion
1 tablespoon chopped green capsicum
2 green chillies
2 teaspoons fresh ginger, grated
3 cloves garlic
½ lb (225g) lean minced lamb, minced twice
1 teaspoon salt
1 teaspoon garam masala
pinch red chilli powder
1 tablespoon finely chopped green coriander
1 teaspoon red food colouring

Blend the egg, onion, capsicum, chillies, ginger and garlic in an electric blender until smooth.

Pour into a bowl and add all the remaining ingredients and mix thoroughly.

Preheat oven to maximum temperature.

Divide mixture into eight equal parts, and using floured hands, form into sausage shapes about 4 inches (10cm) in length.

Place these on a rack in a shallow baking tray and cook near the top of the oven for 10–12 minutes.

Serve, sizzling if liked, with a green salad, lemon wedges and yoghurt mint sauce (recipe page 17).

LAMB TIKKA

The meat for this dish must be very lean. From a whole leg of lamb cut thick succulent strips from the thigh section to reserve for lamb tikka. If you are buying lamb solely for this purpose you will require approximately 12 oz (350g) of lean meat for four persons.

Preparation and cooking time: 30 minutes. (Excludes marinating time).

Serves 4

12 oz (350g) lean lamb taken from the leg
1 cup of tandoori marinade

Cut lamb into 16 strips about ¼ inch (0.5cm) thick and 1½ inches (4cm) wide by 2½ inches (6cm) in length (or into 16 equal size pieces, if this is difficult). Wash the meat and drain, squeezing out excess moisture.

Place the lamb pieces and the marinade in a bowl and mix thoroughly. Cover and refrigerate for 4–6 hours or a maximum of 3 days.

Preheat oven to maximum temperature.

Take the lamb pieces out of the bowl and shake off excess marinade. Arrange them on a rack in a large shallow baking tray, in a single layer.

Cook for 15–20 minutes.

Serve immediately, on a sizzler dish if preferred, with a green salad, lemon wedges and yoghurt mint sauce (recipe page 17).

Note: If you wish to serve lamb tikka as a main course allow eight pieces of meat per person.

CHICKEN TIKKA

Delicious tender chunks of chicken are produced following this recipe, lightly spiced but absolutely oozing with
flavour.

Preparation and cooking time: 20 minutes. (Excludes
marinating time).

Serves 4

3 large chicken fillets
4 tablespoons plain yoghurt
½ teaspoon red chilli powder
½ teaspoon salt
2 teaspoons cooking oil
pinch of yellow food colouring

Cut each chicken fillet into 6 equal size chunks. Wash
and drain.
Place all remaining ingredients into a bowl and mix
well.
Add the chicken pieces to the bowl and mix again
making sure all the pieces are well coated with the
yoghurt.
Cover and refrigerate for 4–6 hours or a maximum of 3
days.
Preheat oven to maximum temperature.
Place chicken pieces onto a rack in a shallow baking
tray in a single layer.
Bake near top of oven for 10 minutes or until cooked
through.
Serve immediately, sizzling if preferred, with a green
salad, wedges of lemon and yoghurt mint sauce (page 17).

TANDOORI FISH

We use cod for this but you may use any white fish that you prefer, such as skate or whiting. Ask the fishmonger to remove all the skin including the white skin.

Preparation and cooking time: 15 minutes. (Excludes marinating time.)

Serves 4

12 oz (350g) skinned white fish
1 cup tandoori marinade

Wash the fish and cut into equal size chunks, about 1 inch (2.5cm) square.

Put the marinade in a bowl and immerse the fish pieces in it ensuring that all of them become coated with the marinade.

Cover and refrigerate for 4–6 hours or a maximum of 24 hours.

Preheat your oven to its maximum temperature.

Remove the fish pieces from the marinade, shaking off any excess. Place them on a rack in a shallow baking tray in a single layer.

Bake near the top of the oven for 7–8 minutes.

Serve immediately with a green salad, lemon wedges and yoghurt mint sauce (recipe page 17).

Note: Instead of baking you may grill the fish pieces under a hot grill, without turning, for 6–7 minutes.

TANDOORI KING PRAWNS

We always buy frozen uncooked prawns still in their shells for this mouthwatering starter. Ready cooked prawns are not suitable.

Preparation and cooking time: 15 minutes.

Serves 4

16 King prawns
1 cup tandoori marinade

Remove shells and beards from prawns, wash and drain.

In a bowl, mix together the prawns and the marinade making sure that the prawns are all well coated.

There is no need to marinate these for long and in fact they should not be left for more than a few minutes.

Preheat your oven to the maximum temperature.

Remove prawns from the marinade shaking off excess, and place on a rack in a shallow baking tray.

Bake near the top of the oven for 7–8 minutes.

Serve, sizzling on a sizzler dish if liked, with a green salad, lemon slices, and yoghurt mint sauce (page 17).

Note: Instead of baking, the prawns may be grilled under a very hot grill for about 5 minutes, turning once.

Allow appropriately increased quantities if you wish to serve tandoori prawns as a main course dish.

CHICKEN CHAT

Chicken that has been prepared using the method for preparation of chicken for curries (page 49) is ideal for this tangy refreshing starter. However, if you are not planning to make any of the curry dishes that require this particular method of preparation, you may cook the chicken using either of the following methods.

1. (microwave) Wash chicken fillets and cut each one into eight equal sized pieces. Toss the chicken in 1 tablespoon of oil to which has been added ½ teaspoon of salt, a pinch of turmeric and a pinch of garam masala. Microwave on high heat for 10–15 minutes according to the instructions for your microwave.

Allow the chicken to cool completely before proceeding with the recipe.

2. (saucepan) Wash and cut chicken pieces as described in (1) above. Put 3 tablespoons of oil, ½ teaspoon of salt, a pinch of turmeric, and a pinch of garam masala into a saucepan. Heat the oil for a few seconds until spices begin to froth, and add the chicken. Stir and cook covered on a low heat for 10–15 minutes, or until chicken is cooked, stirring occasionally.

Drain off the oil and allow the chicken to cool completely before making into chat.

Serves 4

Preparation time: 10 minutes

2 chicken fillets cooked as suggested
1 teaspoon French mustard
2 tablespoons olive oil
1 teaspoon chat masala
2 tablespoons lemon juice
¼ teaspoon salt
¼ teaspoon garam masala
1 teaspoon finely chopped green coriander

To serve: **lettuce, tomato and cucumber**

Cut each chunk of chicken again into four pieces and put into a bowl.

Place all the remaining ingredients into a screw top jar and shake to mix. Alternatively, put them into a bowl and beat with a spoon.

Pour the dressing over the chicken, stir gently, and divide into four portions.

Serve on a bed of shredded lettuce garnished with sliced tomato and cucumber.

ALOO CHAT

This is a cool refreshing starter suitable for vegetarians.

Preparation and cooking time: 35 minutes.

Serves 4

2 medium sized potatoes
1 teaspoon French mustard
2 tablespoons olive oil
1 teaspoon chat masala
2 tablespoons lemon juice
¼ teaspoon salt
¼ teaspoon garam masala
1 teaspoon finely chopped green coriander

To serve: **lettuce, tomato and cucumber.**

Cook potatoes, in their jackets, in boiling salted water until soft. Drain and allow to cool.

Meanwhile put all the remaining ingredients into a screw top jar and shake well to mix, or put them into a bowl and beat with a spoon.

Peel the potatoes and cut into ½ inch (1cm) dice. Place them in a bowl and pour dressing over.

Divide into four portions and serve on a bed of shredded lettuce, garnished with sliced tomato and cucumber.

ONION BHAJEE

A popular starter amongst vegetarians and meat eaters alike, onion bhajees can also be served as a teatime snack.

Preparation and cooking time: 15 minutes

Serves 4

4 medium sized onions
8 oz (225g) gram flour
4 level teaspoons of salt
2 tablespoons mint sauce
1 teaspoon of garam masala
1 teaspoon of finely chopped green coriander
Oil for deep frying

Peel, wash and thinly slice the onions.

Sift the gram flour and salt into a bowl and add enough cold water to make a stiff batter.

Add the onions and all the remaining ingredients to the batter and mix well.

Drop tablespoons of the mixture into hot oil and fry for about three minutes.

Remove the bhajees from the oil and press into circular flat patti shapes.

Return to the oil and cook for a further 2–3 minutes until the outside is a dark brown.

Serve with a green salad and yoghurt mint sauce (recipe page 17).

5

Breads

MENU

NAN – A flat leavened bread that is light and soft with a slightly crisp exterior.

ONION KULCHA – A nan bread to which onion and spices have been added. Masala Kulcha is a similar one with vegetables.

KEEMA NAN – A nan bread with spiced minced lamb spread onto one surface.

PARATHA – A square, flat unleavened bread made with a wholemeal or wheatmeal dough that is layered with butter.

CHAPPATI – A round flat unleavened bread made with wholemeal or wheatmeal flour.

BHATOORA – Very soft, round breads made with a yoghurt dough that is deep fried.

The above are some of the many kinds of bread served in Indian Restaurants, and there are many more kinds which are not. Although the nan breads are the most familiar and perhaps the most popular, I have included recipes for a few others which are very good eaten with Indian curries, bhajees and yoghurts. In some instances they are also easier to make at home, with a little practice.

A variety of flours are used to make such breads, ranging from those flours made from various grains to those made from grinding pulses.

For my recipes you will require only two kinds of flour. One is ordinary white flour, the other is a finely ground wholemeal flour called ata or chappati flour. This is often sold in large bags, but if you can get it in the quantities you want, by all means buy it. If not, buy wholemeal flour and mix it with about 1 cup of plain white flour to 3 cups of the wholemeal. This gives the dough the softness and pliability required for our breads.

EQUIPMENT AND UTENSILS

Breads such as nans are best made in a tandoor which is the name given to a clay oven. At home, a heavy baking tray, a very hot oven and a hot grill will give good results.

Some of our breads such as the bhatoora are deep fried. The best utensil for deep frying is the karahi, a utensil similar to the Chinese wok but deeper and more rounded. A chip pan or deep frying pan will suffice if you do not own a karahi.

Breads such as chappatis and parathas are cooked on tavas. These are slightly concave, cast-iron plates, and the nearest thing to them would be a heavy cast-iron frying pan.

QUICK RECIPE NAN

Although I refer to this as a quick recipe it is by no means a short cut, but a recipe without yeast, which, of course eliminates the time required for proving. Even so, this recipe produces wonderfully light, fluffy nan breads which are best eaten immediately. The yeast recipe given later also produces a delicious nan. It requires a little more time but the breads are more suitable for reheating.

For 6 nans

Preparation and cooking time: 30 minutes approx.

1 lb (450g) S.R. flour plus extra for dusting
½ teaspoon salt

Quick Recipe Nan ingredients (contd.)
½ teaspoon baking powder
2 tablespoons vegetable oil
4 tablespoons plain yoghurt beaten
2 eggs beaten
¼ pint (150ml) water approx.
A little melted vegetable ghee

Sift the flour, salt and baking powder into a bowl. Add the oil, yoghurt and eggs and mix in with a fork.

Now add the water little by little, and using your hands, bring the flour together to make a soft dough.

Knead the dough with damp hands for a minute or two until it is smooth; cover it and leave to rest for at least 15 minutes.

Meanwhile pre-heat the oven to the highest temperature. Put a heavy baking tray to heat in the oven, and pre-heat your grill.

Divide the dough into 6 equal portions. Dust your hands and taking one portion, roll it into a ball in the palms of your hands.

Roll the ball out into a tear shape, or a round if you prefer.

Carefully take the hot baking tray out of the oven, slap the nan onto it and return immediately to the hot oven for about 3 minutes.

Remove the baking tray and the nan from the oven and place them under a hot grill for about 30 seconds to brown lightly and crisp the top.

Brush the top with the melted ghee and wrap in a clean napkin or teatowel and keep warm.

Repeat the process with all the remaining dough. Make two nans at a time if the size of your baking tray and grill will permit.

Serve immediately.

YEAST RECIPE NANS

Makes 6 nans

Preparation and cooking time: 30 minutes, plus an hour to prove the dough

¼ pint (150ml) milk (hand hot)
2 tablespoons caster sugar
2 tablespoons dried active yeast
1 lb (450g) plain flour plus extra for dusting
½ teaspoon salt
1 teaspoon baking powder
2 tablespoons vegetable oil
¼ pint (5 fl.oz) plain yoghurt, beaten
1 large egg, beaten
A little melted vegetable ghee

Pour the milk into a bowl and stir in the sugar and yeast. Set aside for about 15 minutes until the mixture is frothy.

Sift the flour, salt and baking powder into another bowl. Add to it the yeast mixture and all the remaining ingredients (except the ghee), and mix to a dough.

Place the dough on to a clean surface and knead it for 10 minutes or so, until it is smooth.

Put the dough in a greased bowl, cover with greased cling film and set aside in a warm place for about an hour. The dough should double in size.

Knead the dough again lightly before proceeding to make the nans as described in the previous recipe.

KEEMA NAN
These require a little of the mixture for seekh kebabs (page 28) to be spread thinly on the surface of each nan before placing in the oven.

ONION KULCHA
Here thinly sliced onions are pressed into the nans before baking.

For 6 kulchas, thinly slice 2 onions, sprinkle with salt and leave to stand for about an hour.

Drain off the liquid and pat dry with kitchen paper. Mix

a teaspoon of garam masala and 2 teaspoons of finely
chopped coriander with the onions and use by pressing on
to the surface of each nan before cooking.

MASALA KULCHA

For these a mixture of cooked vegetables is pressed onto
the surface of each nan before cooking. Cooked vegetables such as potatoes, peas and onions are ideal. Just mix
with a little salt and garam masala and they are ready for
use.

CHAPPATIS

These flat round breads are made with ata (sometimes
called chappati flour). Three parts wholemeal flour
combined with one part plain white flour may be used
instead. Mix it with water to a soft, slightly sticky dough
and leave to rest at least 15 minutes before using.

Chappatis are cooked on a tava, that is a circular cast-
iron plate with a long handle. A heavy cast-iron frying pan
would make a suitable substitute.

Practice makes perfect when it comes to chappati
making, so do not be put off if your first efforts are not as
good as you would like. They will taste fine even if they
look less than immaculate.

MAKING CHAPPATIS

Makes 8–10

Preparation and cooking time: 30 minutes approx.

**8 oz chappati flour (225g) with extra for dusting (see pages
    38–39)**
4 fl.oz (110ml) water (very approximately)

Put the flour into a bowl. Add the water a little at a time
and bring the flour together with the fingertips.

As the dough becomes stickier, draw it together with

your hands, adding more water until all the flour is incorporated and you have a soft pliable dough.

Knead the dough with wet hands for a minute or two. Fold into a neat shape, dampen the surface, cover and leave to rest for at least 15 minutes.

Put the tava on the hob to pre-heat on a medium heat.

Roughly divide the dough into 8–10 parts without forming into balls.

Now dust your hands lightly with the extra flour and take a portion of the dough. Roll it between your hands into a ball. If it feels sticky use a little extra flour on your hands.

Put the ball of dough into the flour and press flat, dusting on both sides.

Roll out into a round about 6 inches (15cm) in diameter, dusting when required.

Pick up the chappati, pat between your hands for a few seconds to shake off excess flour, and slap it onto the hot tava.

Let it cook for 30 seconds and turn it over. (If the chappati sticks to the tava, it is not hot enough. If the markings on the chappati are very dark then it is too hot. Adjust as necessary).

Cook for about 30 seconds on the second side, lifting the chappati off the tava and replacing it immediately half way through.

Turn over again, now lift the chappati off the tava and place it directly over a medium flame, moving it about all the time. It will puff up in seconds.

Place the chappati in a clean napkin folding over the top to keep warm.

Repeat with the remaining dough. Stack the chappatis in the napkin as you make them.

Ideally chappatis should be eaten immediately, but if you wish to keep them for later, wrap them in aluminium foil and keep them in a refrigerator. Place, still in foil, in a hot oven for about 20 minutes to re-heat. Alternatively re-heat in a microwave oven.

Freezing: Chappatis freeze well. Stack and wrap in foil

and freeze for up to a month. They may be thawed and reheated without removing the foil.

PARATHAS

These are made with the same flour as chappatis but are layered with ghee before being cooked on the tava with more ghee brushed on to them. Vegetable oil is sometimes used instead of ghee and this is perfectly acceptable although I feel the ghee produces the best flavour. Alternatively you may use butter. This, because of the water content in butter, results in a softer, less crisp paratha which I love. It really is a matter of personal preference and convenience which you use, and you may like to try all three before making up your mind.

Makes 6–8

Preparation and cooking time: 30 minutes approx

8 oz (225g) chappati flour plus extra for dusting (see pages 38–39)
4 fl.oz (110ml) water (approximately)
6 tablespoons melted ghee

Make the dough as for chappatis and leave to rest for 15–30 minutes.

Put the tava or cast-iron frying pan on to a medium heat. Meanwhile divide the dough into 6–8 equal portions.

Take one portion with floured hands and roll into a ball.

Place the ball of dough into the flour and press flat, dusting on both sides.

Roll out into a 6 inch (15cm) round, and brush the surface with melted ghee.

Now fold by taking opposite sides and folding until they meet in the middle. You should have a long rectangular shape.

Brush the top surface again with melted ghee and fold, this time bringing in the ends of the rectangle to meet in the middle.

Brush the dry surface for the final time with melted ghee and fold into half. You should have a square.

Place this in the flour, press flat and roll out into a 8 inch (20cm) square.

Pat between your hands and slap onto the hot tava. Cook for about 30 seconds whilst brushing the top surface liberally with ghee. Turn over.

Again brush the surface uppermost with the ghee and turn over, having given the second side 30 seconds.

Continue to cook the first side for a further 30 seconds whilst brushing more melted ghee on the top surface.

Turn over for the final time and cook for a further few seconds.

Both sides should have reddish brown spots. The frequent turning over ensures even cooking.

Put the paratha on a plate lined with a large piece of aluminium foil. Fold over the foil to keep the paratha warm while you make all the parathas in this way.

Like chappatis, parathas are best eaten immediately but are quite good re-heated.

BHATOORA

These deliciously soft round breads are not usually served in Restaurants, but I have decided to include them because they are ideal cooked in advance and re-heated and also because they are probably the easiest of all the Indian breads to make.

You may make these with white flour or ata.

Makes 8–10

Preparation and cooking time: 30 minutes

8 oz (225g) flour
½ teaspoon baking powder
½ teaspoon salt

Bhatoora ingredients (contd.)
8 fl.oz (220ml) plain yoghurt approx.
Oil for deep frying

Sift the flour, baking powder and salt into a bowl. Slowly add the yoghurt and gather the flour together with your finger tips until you have a soft dough.

Knead lightly and set aside to rest for at least 15 minutes.

Put the oil on to heat on a medium heat. Meanwhile divide the dough into 8 portions without rolling into balls.

Dust your hands with flour and take one of the portions of dough and form into a ball.

Flatten the ball, dust well and roll out into a 7–8 inch (17–20cm) round.

Now turn up the heat under the oil for a minute or two to get it really hot.

Slide the bhatoora carefully into the hot oil. It will sink at first but, if the oil is hot enough, it will rise to the surface in seconds.

Using a slotted spoon, push it back into the oil briefly and then turn it over for a few seconds.

Remove the bhatoora from the oil with a slotted spoon and put it on plate lined with kitchen paper.

Repeat with the remaining dough. Drain the bhatooras well on kitchen paper and either serve immediately or wrap in foil for re-heating later.

Tip: If you are making just a few bhatooras, you may like to roll them all out before frying them.

6

Chicken Curries

MENU

CHICKEN CURRY – Mild, Madras, or Vindaloo.

CHICKEN BHUNA MASALA – Boneless chicken cooked in spices and flavoured with green herbs.

CHICKEN MOGHLAI – Chicken pieces cooked with fruits, egg and herbs in a cream sauce.

CHICKEN DO-PIAZA – Mildly spiced chicken cooked with onions.

CHICKEN KORMA – Chicken cooked with cream and nuts, mildly spiced.

CHICKEN DHANSAK – Chicken and lentils cooked in spices.

CHICKEN SAGWALA – Chicken and spinach cooked in spices.

CHICKEN TIKKA MASALA – Boneless chicken, marinated and cooked, blended in a delicate creamy sauce with herbs and spices.

MAKHAN CHICKEN – Tandoori chicken in a delectable cream sauce.

The right equipment

A Restaurant Chef always uses a large frying pan with deep sides (approx 4 ins or 10cm) for cooking his curries. This is important and results in a large amount of food being in contact with the hot surface at one time and a large surface area for the evaporation of water. Not only does this speed up cooking, but allows a more rapid thickening of the sauces without overcooking the meat, fish or vegetables. If you do not have such a pan already, it is well worth investing in one. Alternatively, use a saucepan large enough to afford you the same benefits.

How to prepare the chicken – basic preparation recipe common to most recipes in this chapter.

For our curries we have always used only breast portions of chicken cooked in a special way. Some Restaurants use the whole chicken, but their methods of boiling and removing the flesh from the bones can leave an unwanted boiled taste and some less savoury bits of meat in the finished dish. I would strongly recommend that you follow my suggestion as the end result is well worth it, and you will be amazed how tender the chicken turns out to be.

Preparation and cooking time: 25 minutes

For 6–8 persons you will require:

5 large chicken breasts (approx 2 lb or 900g with skin and bone removed)
6 tablespoons of vegetable oil
1 teaspoon of turmeric
4 tablespoons of the reserved uncooked curry sauce (see page 20)

With a sharp knife remove all fat and membranes from chicken portions and cut each into 8 equal sized pieces. Wash and drain.

Place all the remaining ingredients in a large saucepan and mix well.

Cook on medium heat, stirring continuously until sauce begins to darken in colour (approx. 4–5 mins).

Add the chicken and stir until all the pieces are well coated with the sauce.

Turn down the heat and continue cooking with the lid on for 15–20 minutes, or until chicken is tender, stirring frequently.

Remove chicken pieces (leaving behind the sediment) and place them in a clean container. The cooked chicken can now be used immediately for many of the chicken curries or cooled and refrigerated for up to 4 days.

Freezing: Freeze for up to 2 months.

How to make the curries

Making the curries once you have the sauce is extremely easy. However, read this page carefully as there are a few points you need to know.

In all the following recipes I have allowed for 3–4 servings. If you have frozen half of the sauce and meat after following my recipes on pages 21 and 49, your next Indian meal will be as quick and simple as going to your favourite Restaurant, and just as delicious. If you wish to cater for twice this number, then using the full quantity of sauce will permit you to make two different main dishes, or one main dish and two vegetable, or side dishes as they are known in Indian Restaurants. You could of course make an even greater variety of dishes if you want, bearing in mind that my recipe for curry sauce is enough for up to eight main course dishes.

You may feel that the amount of oil in my recipes seems large. If this is the case, do not be tempted to reduce it at the cooking stage, but instead skim off the top of the finished curry. A generous quantity of oil is essential to bring out the flavour of the spices, and create the right texture in the sauce.

One more point, and that is about food colourings. Indian Restaurants use liberal amounts of red and yellow food colourings. While these are not important to the actual flavour of the food, they make an enormous difference to its appearance. Also, the public is used to particular dishes being a certain colour and some people are not pleased if their favourite dish is not the colour they expected. I recall an incident when a couple walked out of our Restaurant because the colour of their Chicken Tikka was not the deep red they were used to. Yet they had not eaten a morsel of it! Had they done so, they would have found it to be excellent as it is one dish we are particularly proud of, and our customers would agree! However, if you are not happy using artificial colourings you may use natural ones available from Health Food stores, or omit them altogether.

We tend to use the minimum amount of food colourings, but some dishes (and some people as I have explained) demand them – for instance Tandoori Chicken would not, I am sure, be acceptable if it were any colour other than red. Chicken Tikka Masala is another dish that is expected to be a distinctive colour. For these reasons I have included colourings in my recipes where we would normally use them, but if you are really against them, a little extra paprika and/or turmeric produces good results.

CHICKEN CURRY

This is a basic curry dish that is simple to make requiring little other than the cooked chicken and curry sauce. If you wish to make this into a Chicken Madras use 1 teaspoon of chilli powder. Double this amount and you will get a vindaloo. This recipe serves 3–4.

Preparation and cooking time: 15 minutes approx.

5 tablespoons vegetable oil
¾ pint (425ml) curry sauce (page 20)
1 teaspoon salt
Pinch of chilli powder
1 lb (450g) chicken cooked as on page 49
1 level teaspoon garam masala
½ level teaspoon ground cummin
Pinch ground fenugreek
½ tomato thinly sliced
1 tablespoon finely chopped green coriander

Heat the oil in a large, deep frying pan, add the curry sauce, and bring to the boil.

Without reducing the heat, add the salt, chilli powder and the chicken, and continue cooking for about 5 minutes.

Now turn down the heat and stir in the garam masala, ground cummin and dried fenugreek. Simmer for a further 2–3 minutes.

Put in the sliced tomato and half the coriander and cook for another 2 minutes. Skim off any excess oil and serve sprinkled with the remaining coriander.

A little trick: During the last couple of minutes of cooking, a Restaurant Chef will often stir in a teaspoon or so of the marinade used for Tandoori Chicken. This improves texture and flavour of the sauce as well as improving colour.

CHICKEN BHUNA MASALA

This spicy dish is a firm favourite. Remember, spicy does not necessarily mean hot!

Serves 3–4

Preparation and cooking time: 15–20 minutes

2 oz (50g) mushrooms
½ green capsicum
6 tablespoons vegetable oil
¾ pint (425ml or 3 cups) curry sauce (page 20)
1 lb (450g) chicken cooked as on page 49
1 teaspoon salt
½ teaspoon chilli powder
1 green chilli finely chopped
½ teaspoon red food colouring
1½ teaspoons garam masala
1 teaspoon ground cummin
½ teaspoon dried fenugreek
1 tablespoon finely chopped green coriander

Wash the mushrooms and capsicum and slice thinly. Heat the oil in a large deep frying pan and fry for 4–5 minutes on a medium heat.

Add the curry sauce, chicken, salt, chillies and food colouring. Turn up the heat and bring to the boil. Continue cooking for 5 minutes stirring frequently.

Turn down the heat slightly and stir in the garam masala, ground cummin and fenugreek and cook for a further 5 minutes, stirring now and again.

Spoon off any excess oil and serve sprinkled with green coriander.

CHICKEN MOGHLAI

This is another dish suitable for those who do not like their curries spicy. It has a creamy sauce with egg added to it for more body.

Serves 4

Preparation and cooking time: 15–20 minutes

6 tablespoons vegetable oil
¾ pint (425ml or 3 cups) curry sauce (recipe page 20)
1 lb (450g) chicken cooked as on page 49
1 teaspoon salt
¼ teaspoon yellow food colouring
2 eggs
¼ pint (150ml or 1 cup) single cream
1½ teaspoons garam masala
1 teaspoon ground cummin
4 mango slices, tinned or fresh
1 tablespoon finely chopped green coriander

Heat the oil in a large deep frying pan, add the curry sauce and bring to the boil on a high heat.

Now add the chicken, salt and food colouring. Stir well and continue cooking on a high heat for about 5 minutes stirring regularly.

Now turn down the heat to medium and simmer for a further 5 minutes, stirring occasionally.

Meanwhile whisk the eggs and combine with the cream.

Spoon off any excess oil that will have risen to the surface, and stir in the egg and cream mixture.

Also stir in the garam masala and ground cummin. Continue cooking for a further 2–3 minutes stirring more-or-less continuously.

Serve garnished with mango slices and green coriander.

CHICKEN DO-PIAZA

This is a mildly spiced dish cooked with onions. A delicious variation on the basic chicken curry.

Serves 3–4

Preparation and cooking time: 15 minutes

6 tablespoons vegetable oil
2 small onions peeled and cut into rings
¾ pint (425ml or 3 cups) curry sauce (page 20)
1 teaspoon salt
1 level teaspoon chilli powder
1 lb (450g) chicken cooked as on page 49
1 level teaspoon garam masala
1 level teaspoon ground cummin
½ level teaspoon ground coriander
½ level teaspoon dried fenugreek
1 tablespoon finely chopped green coriander

Heat the oil in a large frying pan. Add the sliced onions and fry until transparent but not starting to brown. Add the curry sauce, mix well and bring to a simmer. Stir in salt, chilli powder and chicken. Cook on medium heat for 10 minutes, or until sauce is quite thick, stirring occasionally.

Now stir in the garam masala, cummin, ground coriander and fenugreek. Continue simmering for 3–4 minutes.

Skim off excess oil and serve sprinkled with coriander.

CHICKEN KORMA

This dish is a deliciously creamy one preferred by those who like their curries mild.

Serves 3–4

Preparation and cooking time: 15 minutes

4 tablespoons vegetable oil
¾ pint (425ml or 3 cups) curry sauce (page 20)
1 lb (450g) chicken cooked as on page 49
2 tablespoons cashew nuts roughly chopped
1½ teaspoons salt
¼ teaspoon yellow food colouring
½ teaspoon garam masala
1 teaspoon ground cummin
¼ pint (150ml or 1 cup) single cream
2 teaspoons finely chopped green coriander

Heat the oil in a large, deep frying pan and add to it the curry sauce. Bring to the boil on a high heat.

Do not reduce the heat. Put in the chicken, cashew nuts, salt and food colouring. Stir, and cook for 5 minutes or so stirring regularly.

Turn down the heat slightly and continue to cook for a further 5 minutes. Stir in the garam masala and ground cummin.

Now stir in the cream and heat gently for 3–4 minutes, stirring all the time.

Serve sprinkled with the green coriander.

CHICKEN DHANSAK

This variation combines chicken with lentil dal. It requires less curry sauce because of this and is a tasty dish for those who like the flavour of lentils. This is a hot, sour dish to which you could also add pineapple chunks if you want.

Serves 3–4

Preparation and cooking time: 15–20 minutes

6 tablespoons vegetable oil
½ pint (275ml or 2 cups) curry sauce (page 20)
2 cups lentil dal (recipe page 92)
1 lb (450g) chicken cooked as on page 49
½ teaspoon salt
½ teaspoon chilli powder
1 green chilli finely chopped
1½ teaspoons garam masala
1 teaspoon ground cummin
2 tablespoons lemon juice
1 tablespoon finely chopped green coriander

Heat the oil in a large deep frying pan, add the curry sauce and lentils and bring to the boil.

Without turning down the heat, put in the chicken, salt, chilli powder and green chilli.

Stir well and continue to cook on high heat for about 5 minutes, or until sauce thickens, stirring regularly.

Now turn down the heat to a simmer for a further 5 minutes. Stir occasionally.

Skim off any excess oil and stir in the garam masala, ground cummin and lemon juice.

Serve sprinkled with the green coriander.

CHICKEN SAGWALA

This is an unusual but tasty combination of chicken and spinach.

Serves 4

Preparation and cooking time: 20–25 minutes

6 tablespoons oil
¾ pint (425ml or 3 cups) curry sauce (page 20)
16 oz (450g) can puréed spinach
1 teaspoon salt
1 teaspoon chilli powder
1 green chilli finely chopped (optional)
1 lb (450g) chicken cooked as on page 49
1½ teaspoons garam masala
2 teaspoons finely chopped green coriander

Heat the oil in a large deep frying pan, add the curry sauce and spinach, stir and bring to the boil.

Stir in the salt, chilli powder and green chilli and continue to cook until the mixture becomes quite thick. This takes about 10–15 minutes and the oil should start to separate when this is right. Stir frequently and ensure that it does not stick to the pan.

Now put in the chicken and the garam masala and simmer on a very low heat for a further 5 minutes, stirring now and again.

Take off the heat, stir in the coriander and serve.

CHICKEN TIKKA MASALA

A delicious, slightly creamy, medium spiced dish made with chicken tikka.

Serves 3–4

Preparation and cooking time: 15 minutes

4 tablespoons vegetable oil
¾ pint (425ml or 3 cups) curry sauce (recipe page 20)
1 teaspoon paprika
1 teaspoon salt
1 level teaspoon chilli powder
Pinch red food colouring
1 teaspoon garam masala
½ teaspoon ground cummin
3 chicken fillets freshly made into chicken tikka (page 30)
6 tablespoons single cream
1 tablespoon finely chopped green coriander

Heat the oil in a large deep frying pan, add the curry sauce and bring to the boil.

Without reducing the heat add the paprika, salt, chilli powder and food colouring. Cook for 5 minutes stirring frequently, or until sauce thickens.

Turn down the heat and put in the garam masala and cummin powder. Stir. Cook for 3 minutes.

Cut each piece of chicken tikka into two smaller pieces, stir them in, with the cream, into the sauce and simmer for a further 2–3 minutes.

Serve sprinkled with the green coriander.

MAKHAN CHICKEN

This is a fairly simple but quite spectacular dish in which Tandoori Chicken (recipe page 27) is transformed by a delectable creamy sauce.

Serves 4

Preparation and cooking time: 30 minutes

2 oz (50g) butter, preferably unsalted
½ pint (275ml or 2 cups) curry sauce (page 20)
2 tablespoons tomato purée
1 level teaspoon garam masala
½ teaspoon salt
½ teaspoon ground cummin
1 green chilli finely chopped
1 tablespoon finely chopped green coriander
3 teaspoons lemon juice
½ pint (275ml) single cream
4 portions freshly cooked Tandoori Chicken

Melt the butter in a large frying pan with deep sides. Add the curry sauce, tomato purée, garam masala, salt, cummin, chilli, coriander and lemon juice. Mix well.

Bring to a simmer and cook on medium heat for a minute or so, mixing in the butter as you do so.

Stir in the cream, cook for another minute and add the chicken pieces.

Stir once and serve.

7

YOGHURT

Lamb Curries

MENU

LAMB CURRY – Mild, Madras, or Vindaloo.

BHUNA GHOST – Lamb cooked in spices and flavoured with green herbs.

LAMB PASANDA – Marinated lamb pieces in a mild creamy sauce with nuts.

LAMB DO-PIAZA – Lamb cooked with onions and spices.

SHAHI KORMA – Lamb cooked in cream, spices and nuts, mildly spiced.

ROGAN JOSH – Lamb cooked with yoghurt, spices and nuts.

LAMB DHANSAK – Lamb with lentils.

SAG MEAT – Lamb cooked with spinach and spices.

KEEMA PEAS – Minced lamb cooked with spices and peas.

PREPARATION OF LAMB

Lamb is generally the only red meat used by Indian Restaurants. The use of beef or pork is largely avoided, as certain ethnic groups will not eat one or the other.

For our lamb curries we use leg of spring lamb, either fresh or frozen, according to season. The quality of your lamb dishes will depend heavily on the quality and preparation of the meat. It is essential to buy tender spring lamb and remove – or have removed by your butcher – all bone, fat and gristle. Cut the remaining lean meat into one inch (2.5cm) cubes (except for *Lamb Pasanda*) and you are ready to proceed.

NB. – All the recipes in this book are for boned lamb. If you prefer your meat unboned you may use it this way, but remember to double the quantity.

Preparation and cooking time: 45 minutes.

For 6–8 persons you will need:

2 lbs (900g) lamb prepared as above
8 tablespoons vegetable oil
1 teaspoon turmeric
4 tablespoons reserved uncooked curry sauce

Wash and drain meat. Place remaining ingredients in a large saucepan and mix well. Cook on medium heat, stirring continuously until sauce begins to darken in colour (4–5 mins). Add the meat and stir until all the pieces are well coated. Turn down the heat and cook covered for 30–40 minutes or until meat is tender, stirring every few minutes to ensure even cooking.

Remove lamb pieces, leaving behind the sediment, and place in clean container. The lamb may now be used immediately for any of the curries in this chapter, as well as *Lamb Biryani* (but not for *Balti Meat*).

Or it can be cooled and refrigerated for up to 4 days. If refrigerating, skim the oil from the sediment and pour onto meat to keep moist.

Freezing: Freeze for up to 2 months.

LAMB CURRY

This is a basic lamb curry that is simple to make. Vary the chilli according to taste for a mild to medium to very hot curry, or use a combination of chilli powder and green chillies for more flavour.

Serves 3–4

Preparation and cooking time: 15 minutes

5 tablespoons vegetable oil
¾ pint (425ml or 3 cups) curry sauce (page 20)
1 teaspoon salt
½ teaspoon chilli powder
1 lb (450g) cooked lamb (page 63)
1 level teaspoon garam masala
½ level teaspoon ground cummin
Pinch ground fenugreek
1 tablespoon finely chopped green coriander

Heat the oil in a large, deep frying pan, add the curry sauce and bring to the boil.

Continue to cook on a high heat and add the salt, chilli powder and the cooked lamb. Mix well and cook for about 5 minutes.

Turn down the heat to a simmer and stir in the garam masala, ground cummin and dried fenugreek. Simmer for a further 6-7 minutes.

Skim off any excess oil. Sprinkle on the coriander just before serving.

BHUNA GHOST

This is a delicious spicy lamb dish and a firm favourite. Vary the "heat" according to taste.

Serves 3–4

Preparation and cooking time: 15–20 minutes

2 oz (50g) mushrooms
½ green capsicum
6 tablespoons vegetable oil
¾ pint (425ml or 3 cups) curry sauce (page 20)
1 lb (450g) cooked lamb (page 63)
1 teaspoon salt
½ teaspoon chilli powder
1 green chilli finely chopped
¼ teaspoon red food colouring
1½ teaspoons garam masala
1 teaspoon ground cummin
½ teaspoon dried fenugreek
1 tablespoon finely chopped green coriander

Wash the mushrooms and capsicum and slice thinly. Heat the oil in a large deep frying pan and fry for 4-5 minutes on a medium heat.

Add the curry sauce, lamb, salt, chillies and food colouring. Turn up the heat and bring to the boil. Continue cooking for 5 minutes stirring frequently.

Now turn down the heat slightly and stir in the garam masala, ground cummin and fenugreek and cook for a further 5 minutes, stirring now and again.

Spoon off excess oil and sprinkle on the green coriander before serving.

LAMB PASANDA

The lamb for this dish will need to be prepared in advance as it requires marinating. Will serve 3 or 4.

Preparation and cooking time: 35–40 minutes

1 lb (450g) lean lamb
½ teaspoon salt
1 cup plain yoghurt
4 tablespoons vegetable oil
¾ pint (425ml or 3 cups) curry sauce (page 20)
1 teaspoon each, salt and paprika
½ teaspoon garam masala
1 teaspoon ground cummin
1 tablespoon roughly chopped cashew nuts (optional)
4 tablespoons double cream
1 tablespoon finely chopped green coriander

Wash the meat and cut into slices about a ¼ inch (0.5cm) thick and 3 inches (7.5cm) by 2 inches (5cm). Boil in salted water for 15 minutes or until the meat is tender.

Mix the yoghurt and salt in a bowl and put in the meat slices whilst still hot. Stir, coating the meat well and marinate for at least 2 hours or up to 24 hours.

Heat the oil in a large deep frying pan, pour in the sauce and bring it to the boil. Stir in the salt and paprika and cook on a high heat for 5 minutes, stirring frequently.

Now turn down the heat and stir in the garam masala, cummin and nuts. Also add the meat, shaking off as much of the yoghurt as you can. Stir and simmer for 5 minutes or so.

Spoon off any oil and stir in the cream and half the coriander. Simmer for a minute.

Sprinkle the remaining coriander on top just before serving.

LAMB DO-PIAZA

This is a mildly spiced lamb dish cooked with onions.

Serves 3–4

Preparation and cooking time: 15 minutes

6 tablespoons vegetable oil
2 small onions peeled and cut into rings
¾ pint (425ml or 3 cups) curry sauce (page 20)
1 teaspoon salt
1 level teaspoon chilli powder
1 lb (450g) cooked lamb (page 63)
1 level teaspoon garam masala
1 level teaspoon ground cummin
½ level teaspoon ground coriander
½ level teaspoon dried fenugreek
1 tablespoon finely chopped green coriander

Heat the oil in a large frying pan. Add the sliced onions and fry until transparent. Pour in the curry sauce, mix well and bring to a simmer.

Stir in salt, chilli powder and lamb. Cook on medium heat for 10 minutes, or until sauce is quite thick, stirring now and again.

Now stir in the garam masala, cummin, ground coriander and fenugreek. Continue to cook for 3–4 minutes.

Skim off excess oil and sprinkle with green coriander before serving.

SHAHI KORMA

This is a delicious creamy lamb dish.

Serves 3–4

Preparation and cooking time: 15 minutes

4 tablespoons vegetable oil
¾ pint (425ml or 3 cups) curry sauce (page 20)
1 lb (450g) cooked lamb (page 63)
2 tablespoons cashew nuts roughly chopped
1½ teaspoons salt
¼ teaspoon yellow food colouring
½ teaspoon garam masala
1 teaspoon ground cummin
¼ pint (150ml or 1 cup) single cream
2 teaspoons finely chopped green coriander

Heat the oil in a large, deep frying pan and add to it the curry sauce. Bring to the boil on a high heat.

Without turning down the heat, put in the lamb, cashew nuts, salt and food colouring. Stir, and cook for 5 minutes or so stirring frequently.

Turn down the heat slightly and continue to cook for a further 5 minutes. Stir in the garam masala and ground cummin.

Now stir in the cream and heat gently for 3–4 minutes, stirring all the time.

Serve sprinkled with the green coriander.

ROGAN JOSH

This is probably the most popular of all the lamb dishes.

Serves 3–4

Preparation and cooking time: 15 minutes

6 tablespoons vegetable oil
¾ pint (425ml or 3 cups) curry sauce (page 20)
1 lb (450g) cooked lamb (page 63)
2 teaspoons paprika
1 teaspoon chilli powder
1 teaspoon salt
1 tablespoon cashew nuts (optional)
1 teaspoon garam masala
1 teaspoon ground cummin
2 tablespoons plain yoghurt, beaten smooth
2 teaspoons finely chopped green coriander

Heat the oil in a large deep frying pan, add to it the curry sauce and bring to the boil.

Without reducing the heat, put in the meat, paprika, chilli powder, salt and cashew nuts (if used). Stir well and cook for 5 minutes stirring frequently.

Now turn down the heat and whilst the meat is simmering, stir in the garam masala and ground cummin. Slowly add the yoghurt, mixing all the time and cooking for a further 3 or 4 minutes. There should now be a dark thick sauce reddish brown in colour.

Allow to settle and spoon off any excess oil. Serve sprinkled with the green coriander.

LAMB DHANSAK

This is a lamb curry combined with lentil dal. A hot, sour dish, it sometimes has pineapple chunks added to it. Stir these in just before serving if you wish to try it this way.

Serves 3–4

Preparation and cooking time: 15–20 minutes

6 tablespoons vegetable oil
½ pint (275ml or 2 cups) curry sauce (page 20)
2 cups lentil dal (page 92)
1 lb (450g) cooked lamb (page 63)
½ teaspoon salt
½ teaspoon chilli powder
1 green chilli finely chopped
1½ teaspoons garam masala
1 teaspoon ground cummin
2 tablespoons lemon juice
1 tablespoon finely chopped green coriander

Heat the oil in a large deep frying pan, add the curry sauce and lentil dal and bring to the boil.

Without turning down the heat, add the lamb, salt, chilli powder and green chilli.

Stir well and continue to cook on a high heat for about 5 minutes, or until sauce thickens, stirring regularly.

Now turn down the heat to a simmer for a further 5 minutes, stirring now and again.

Skim off any excess oil and stir in the garam masala, ground cummin and lemon juice.

Serve sprinkled with green coriander.

SAG MEAT

This dish is an interesting combination of lamb and spinach.

Serves 4

Preparation and cooking time: 20–25 minutes

6 tablespoons vegetable oil
¾ pint (425ml or 3 cups) curry sauce (page 20)
16 oz (450g) can puréed spinach
1 teaspoon salt
1 teaspoon chilli powder
1 green chilli finely chopped (optional)
1 lb (450g) cooked lamb (page 63)
1½ teaspoons garam masala
2 teaspoons finely chopped green coriander

Heat the oil in a large deep frying pan, add the curry sauce and spinach, stir and bring to the boil.

Stir in the salt, chilli powder, and green chilli (if used) and continue to cook until the mixture thickens, stirring frequently. This will take about 10–15 minutes.

Now put in the lamb and the garam masala and simmer on a low heat for a further 5 minutes, stirring now and again.

Take off the heat before stirring in the coriander.

KEEMA PEAS

This is a dish consisting of lean minced lamb and garden peas.

Serves 4

Preparation and cooking time: 40–45 minutes

4 tablespoons vegetable oil
1 lb (450g) minced lamb
½ pint (275ml or 2 cups) curry sauce (page 20)
½ lb (225g) frozen peas
1 teaspoon salt
1 teaspoon ground cummin
½ teaspoon chilli powder
½ green chilli finely chopped
1 teaspoon garam masala
2 teaspoons finely chopped green coriander

Heat the oil in a pan on a medium heat, add the minced lamb and cook, stirring until browned. Turn down the heat and cook covered for 10 minutes.

Now add the curry sauce, peas, salt, ground cummin, chilli powder and green chilli. Stir and bring the sauce to a simmer. Continue to simmer uncovered for about 30 minutes.

Stir in the garam masala and cook for a minute. Take off the heat before stirring in the green coriander.

Balti Dishes

MENU

BALTI CHICKEN

BALTI MEAT

I can think of few things in Indian cookery more mouthwatering than the delicious sound of a sizzling tandoori starter or balti curry. Although the concept of the balti dish is simple, its allure is remarkable. That unmistakable sizzle and aroma as you are served your meal still simmering from the kitchen in its individual balti, makes these dishes exceptionally popular. And so they should be. With a generous combination of succulent pieces of meat or chicken, onions and capsicums, all smothered in a dark, thick and spicy sauce, these dishes are among the best from the Restaurant menu.

The balti is another name for the Indian karahi, a utensil similar to the Chinese wok. The sizzle is produced by putting the hot curry into a pre-heated balti. The oily sauce comes into contact with the hot surface and causes the sizzling.

You will need to buy the baltis or karahis if you wish to serve these dishes in the traditional way. It is not of course essential, but you will require them if you want authenticity. Baltis can be found in many Indian and Pakistani stores and are relatively inexpensive to buy. In their absence any metal utensil such as a small frying pan or saucepan would do.

BALTI CHICKEN

Serves 2–3

Preparation and cooking time: 20–25 minutes

3 Chicken fillets
4 tablespoons vegetable oil plus more for deep frying
¾ pint (425ml or 3 cups) curry sauce (page 20)
Red food colouring (optional)
1 teaspoon salt
½ teaspoon chilli powder
1 medium sized onion
1 green capsicum
1½ teaspoons garam masala
1 teaspoon ground cummin
1 tablespoon finely chopped green coriander

Cut each chicken fillet into 4 strips, wash and drain.

Heat the oil in a large deep pan and put the chicken pieces into it. Sauté for 4–5 minutes on medium heat.

Pour the curry sauce into the pan with the chicken and bring to the boil on a high heat. Turn down the heat to medium.

Now add the food colouring, salt and chilli powder. Stir and leave to simmer for 12–15 minutes, stirring now and again.

Meanwhile, peel and wash the onion. Slice into two halves and then quarter each half. Set aside.

Wash the capsicum, slice lengthways into two and deseed. Now cut each half into two strips and each strip into three pieces across.

Heat the oil for deep frying. When hot put in it the onion and capsicum. Fry for 2–3 minutes until the onion is just beginning to brown. Remove with a slotted spoon and drain on kitchen paper.

When the chicken has been simmering for 12 minutes or so, add to it the fried onion and capsicum.

Continue cooking on a medium heat until the sauce becomes quite thick, about 5 minutes or so.

Stir in the garam masala and ground cummin and turn the heat to very low. The oil will start to rise to the surface where it can be skimmed off if desired.

While the chicken is still on a low heat, heat the baltis. This can be done on top of the hob for about 30 seconds.

When you have done this, immediately spoon in the curry. It will start sizzling and simmering in the balti.

Quickly sprinkle on the green coriander and serve.

NB. If you do not get the sizzling when you put the curry in the baltis, it is probably because you have not heated them sufficiently. They need to be quite hot and not just warm. Leave the curry simmering while you heat the baltis. It is the combination of the piping hot curry and very hot balti that causes the sizzling.

BALTI MEAT

Follow the recipe for Balti Chicken, replacing the chicken with 1 lb (450g) cooked lamb for 2–3 persons. You will not need to sauté the cooked meat, so omit that stage of the method and simply put the sauce and meat into the hot oil and proceed from there.

It will be necessary for you to read page 62 on how to prepare lamb, but remember that there is a larger quantity of meat in balti meat than other curries and allow approximately 1 lb (450g) of lean meat for 2 or 3 people, instead of for 3 or 4 as in other recipes. Also when cutting the meat into cubes make them a little larger than the 1 inch (2.5cm) recommended. This is ideal but not essential, so if you have some cooked lamb in the freezer that you have kept for curries, you may use it in balti meat.

Fish Curries

MENU

PRAWN CURRY

BHUNA PRAWN

PRAWN AND MUSHROOM

TANDOORI KING PRAWN MASALA

TANDOORI FISH MASALA

Indian Restaurants are often not very adventurous when it comes to fish, relying mainly on prawns for the fish dishes on the menu. I have included these popular prawn dishes in this chapter and also one using cod. You may, however, like to experiment with other varieties such as haddock, plaice or mackerel. Simply remember to cook the fish first and either stir into the sauce of your choice or pour the sauce over the fish just before serving.

A word about prawns. I have said in an earlier chapter that we always buy King prawns that are uncooked and frozen in their shells. Fresh, uncooked prawns appear not to be readily available so this is the next best choice. Using freshly cooked rather than pre-cooked prawns is by far the best way and the difference is quite noticeable. Smaller prawns may be bought pre-cooked but be careful not to over cook them.

PRAWN CURRY

Use King prawns or the smaller variety as you prefer. If using uncooked King prawns, cook them in boiling salted water for 5 minutes and cut each prawn in half.

Remember, you can produce a prawn madras or vindaloo simply by increasing the amount of chilli powder.

Serves 3–4

Preparation and cooking time: 10–15 minutes

4 tablespoons vegetable oil
¾ pint (425ml or 3 cups) curry sauce (page 20)
½ teaspoon salt
Pinch chilli powder or to taste
½ teaspoon ground coriander
12 oz (350g) peeled prawns defrosted as necessary
½ teaspoon garam masala
1 tablespoon finely chopped green coriander

Heat the oil in a large deep frying pan and pour in the curry sauce. Bring to the boil and cook on a medium/high heat for about 5 minutes until you have a thick sauce.

Stir in all the remaining ingredients except for the green coriander and simmer, stirring frequently, for 4 or 5 minutes.

Sprinkle the green coriander over just before serving.

BHUNA PRAWN

This is a spicy prawn dish with a good, thick sauce. Remember to cook uncooked prawns for 5 minutes in boiling salted water and to slice King prawns in two.

Serves 3–4

Preparation and cooking time: 15–20 minutes

2 oz (50g) button mushrooms
½ green capsicum
6 tablespoons vegetable oil
¾ pint (425ml or 3 cups) curry sauce (page 20)
1 teaspoon salt
½ teaspoon chilli powder
1 teaspoon cummin
1½ teaspoons garam masala
12 oz (350g) peeled prawns defrosted as necessary
½ teaspoon dried fenugreek
1 tablespoon finely chopped green coriander

Rinse the mushrooms and capsicum and slice thinly. Heat the oil in a large deep frying pan and fry them for 4–5 minutes on a medium heat.

Now add the curry sauce, salt, chilli powder and cummin. Turn up the heat and bring to the boil.

Cook the sauce on a high heat, stirring frequently, until it is really thick.

Stir in the garam masala, prawns and dried fenugreek and simmer for 3 minutes.

Drain off excess oil and sprinkle with the green coriander before serving.

PRAWN AND MUSHROOM

As with the other prawn dishes in this chapter, use either King prawns or small prawns. Cook uncooked King prawns in boiling salted water for 5 minutes and cut into 2 pieces before using.

Serves 4

Preparation and cooking time: 15–20 minutes

4 oz (110g) button mushrooms
6 tablespoons vegetable oil
¾ pint (425ml or 3 cups) curry sauce (page 20)
1 teaspoon salt
½ teaspoon chilli powder
½ teaspoon ground coriander
12 oz (350g) peeled prawns defrosted as necessary
1 teaspoon garam masala
1 tablespoon finely chopped green coriander

Rinse and halve, quarter or thickly slice the mushrooms according to size.

Heat the oil in a large, deep frying pan and fry the mushrooms on a medium heat for 4 minutes.

Add the curry sauce, salt, chilli powder, and ground coriander.

Bring the sauce to the boil on a high heat and cook for around 5 minutes until thickened.

Now add the prawns and garam masala and simmer gently for 3 minutes.

Drain off excess oil and serve sprinkled with green coriander.

TANDOORI KING PRAWN MASALA AND FISH MASALA

This is a delicious, creamy dish using King prawns that have been cooked tandoori style. It serves 3 or 4.

Preparation and cooking time: 15 minutes

4 tablespoons vegetable oil
¾ pint (425ml or 3 cups) curry sauce (page 20)
1 teaspoon each, salt and paprika
½ teaspoon chilli powder
Pinch red food colouring
1 level teaspoon garam masala
½ teaspoon ground cummin
16 King prawns freshly cooked tandoori style (page 32)
6 tablespoons single cream
1 tablespoon finely chopped green coriander

Heat the oil in a large, deep frying pan, add the curry sauce and bring to the boil.

Add the paprika, salt, chilli powder and food colouring and cook the sauce, stirring, on a medium/high heat for about 5 minutes until it is quite thick.

Reduce the heat and stir in the garam masala and cummin powder. Simmer for 3 minutes.

Spoon off any excess oil. Cut each prawn in half and add them to the sauce. Stir in the cream and heat through for 2 minutes. Serve sprinkled with the green coriander.

TANDOORI FISH MASALA

This dish is made in the same way as Tandoori King Prawn Masala. Substitute the Tandoori King Prawns with Tandoori Fish (page 31), allowing around 12 oz (350g) for 3–4 persons.

10

Vegetable Curries

VEGETABLE CURRIES, BHAJEES and DALS

MENU

BENGAN BHAJEE – Aubergine cooked in spices.

ALOO GOBI – Potatoes and cauliflower in spices.

CHANA ALOO – Chick peas cooked with potatoes.

MUSHROOMS AND PEAS – Mushrooms and peas in a spicy sauce.

BHINDI BHAJEE – Okra cooked with onion and spices.

MIXED VEGETABLES – Fresh garden vegetables with herbs and spices.

TARKA DAL – Lentils with herbs and spices.

SAG PANIR – Spinach with cottage cheese cubes.

MATTAR PANIR – Cottage cheese with peas in a spicy sauce.

BENGAN BHAJEE

Aubergines are best cooked in plenty of hot oil and this dish demands that you do not skimp on the oil during cooking although you may strain it off afterwards.

Buy plump aubergines with an even shiny purple colour.

Serves 4–6

Preparation and cooking time: 30–35 minutes

1 lb (450g) aubergines
1 small green capsicum
1 cooking onion
1 teaspoon salt
½ teaspoon chilli powder
1 teaspoon garam masala
1 cup vegetable oil

Wash and cut the aubergines lengthwise into quarters, and then cut into about 1 inch (2.5cm) thick wedges.

Cut the capsicum in a similar way, and peel and chop the onion coarsely, separating the slices.

Place all the vegetables in a bowl and sprinkle on the salt and spices and mix well.

Heat the oil in a karahi or deep pan. When hot put in the vegetables and cook, stirring frequently on a medium heat for 10 minutes.

Turn down the heat slightly and cook for a further 10–15 minutes until the aubergine wedges are soft but still hold their shape.

Allow the oil to settle for a few minutes and drain off if desired.

Serve hot.

ALOO GOBI

This is a popular dish of cauliflower and potatoes.

Serves 4

Preparation and cooking time: 40–45 minutes

½ lb (225g) potatoes
1 small cauliflower
4 tablespoons vegetable oil
½ teaspoon ground cummin
1 cup curry sauce (page 20)
1 level teaspoon salt
½ teaspoon ground coriander
½ teaspoon turmeric
1 green chilli finely chopped
2 teaspoons finely chopped green coriander

Boil or microwave the potatoes in their jackets and leave until cool enough to handle.

Break up the cauliflower into florets. Rinse and drain.

Heat the oil in a heavy based pan. When hot put in the ground cummin. Almost immediately add the cauliflower. Cook, stirring on a medium heat, for 2–3 minutes.

Now add the curry sauce, salt, ground coriander, turmeric and chilli. Mix well and cook partly covered on a low heat for about 20 minutes or until the cauliflower is just tender. Stir frequently during this time.

Whilst the cauliflower is cooking, peel the potatoes and cut into 1 inch (2.5cm) dice.

Add the potatoes to the cooked cauliflower and stir gently to prevent them breaking. Heat through for 3 or 4 minutes.

Stir in the green coriander and serve.

CHANA ALOO

Chana or chickpeas are available ready cooked in cans from most supermarkets. Many Restaurants buy them this way as they are good and convenient. If you buy them uncooked, they will need to be soaked for about 24 hours and then simmered for about an hour to an hour and a half until tender.

Serves 3–4

Preparation and cooking time: 20–25 minutes

½ lb (225g) potatoes
15 oz (425g) can chickpeas in brine
5 tablespoons vegetable oil
½ pint (275ml or 2 cups) curry sauce (page 20)
2 teaspoons tomato purée
1 teaspoon salt
1 teaspoon ground cummin
1 teaspoon ground coriander
1 teaspoon garam masala
1 teaspoon chilli powder
½ teaspoon ambchoor (or 2 tablespoons lemon juice)
½ teaspoon dried fenugreek
2 teaspoons finely chopped green coriander

Boil or microwave potatoes in their skins. Cool slightly, peel, and cut into 1 inch (2.5cm) dice.

Drain and rinse the chickpeas in a colander.

Heat the oil in a heavy pan, add the curry sauce and boil for about 5 minutes until thickened.

Stir in all the remaining ingredients except the potatoes and green coriander, and simmer gently for 5 minutes, stirring frequently.

Add the potatoes, heat through for 4 or 5 minutes, and stir in the green coriander.

MUSHROOMS AND PEAS

This delicious dish is not often found in Restaurants, but one that is definitely worth trying. Halve, quarter or thickly slice the mushrooms according to their size.

Serves 3–4

Preparation and cooking time: 30 minutes

12 oz (350g) button mushrooms
8 oz (225g) pack frozen peas
4 tablespoons vegetable oil
1½ cups curry sauce (page 20)
1 level teaspoon salt
½ teaspoon turmeric
½ teaspoon ground cummin
½ teaspoon chilli powder
½ teaspoon dried fenugreek
½ teaspoon garam masala
2 teaspoons finely chopped green coriander

Rinse and thickly slice the mushrooms. Rinse the frozen peas well in hot water and drain.

Heat the oil in a deep frying pan. When hot, put in the mushrooms and cook on a gentle heat for 3–4 minutes.

Add the peas and cook for 5 minutes.

Now add the curry sauce and bring to a simmer. Stir in the salt, turmeric, ground cummin and chilli powder.

Simmer, stirring occasionally, for about 15 minutes.

Add the dried fenugreek and the garam masala and simmer for a further 5 minutes.

Allow the oil to settle and skim off the excess. Stir in the green coriander and serve.

BHINDI BHAJEE

This is probably the most popular of the vegetable dishes served in Indian Restaurants.

Buy fresh okra and look for young tender pods.

Serves 4

Preparation and cooking time: 20–25 minutes

12 oz (350g) okra
Oil for deep frying
3 tablespoons vegetable oil
1 cup curry sauce (page 20)
1 level teaspoon salt
½–1 teaspoon chilli powder
1 teaspoon ground cummin
1 teaspoon ground coriander
½ teaspoon garam masala
3 teaspoons lemon juice

Wash the okra and pat dry. Top and tail the pods and cut into about ¾ inch (2cm) lengths.

Heat the oil for deep frying and fry the okra for 7–8 minutes. Drain.

Heat the 3 tablespoons of oil in a deep frying pan and pour in the curry sauce. Bring it to the boil and cook on a high heat until it becomes quite thick.

Turn down the heat and stir in the salt and spices. Add the okra to the pan and mix well.

Cook uncovered for about 3 minutes and sprinkle on the lemon juice.

Serve hot.

MIXED VEGETABLES

Use any combination of carrots, peas, potatoes, cauliflower and green beans. Left over cooked vegetables are suitable for this dish.

Serves 4–6

Preparation and cooking time: 25–30 minutes

1 lb (450g) diced vegetables
3 tablespoons vegetable oil
1½ cups curry sauce (page 20)
1 teaspoon salt
½ teaspoon turmeric
½ teaspoon ground coriander
½ teaspoon garam masala
½ teaspoon chilli powder
2 teaspoons finely chopped green coriander

Cook the vegetables in boiling salted water for 10–15 minutes until just tender. Drain.

Heat the oil in a large frying pan, pour in the curry sauce and bring it to the boil.

Cook for about 5 minutes until the sauce thickens, and turn down the heat.

Stir in the salt and all the spices and add the cooked vegetables. Stir well and cook for 5 minutes.

Sprinkle with the green coriander just before serving.

TARKA DAL

This nutritious dal is made with red split lentils which turn a pale yellow when cooked.

Serves 4–6.

Preparation and cooking time: 1 hour

½ cup red split lentils
3 cups water
1 level teaspoon salt
1 small onion chopped
3 cloves garlic finely chopped
4 tablespoons melted vegetable ghee
Pinch turmeric
½ teaspoon garam masala
1 small tomato
2 teaspoons finely chopped green coriander

Pick over the lentils for any stones and wash them in several changes of water. Put into a saucepan with the 3 cups of water, add the salt and bring to the boil.

Turn down the heat and simmer uncovered, skimming off the froth that collects at the top for the first 20 minutes or so of cooking. After this stage, the pan should be partly covered.

Cook, stirring occasionally, for a total of 1 hour, at the end of which time you will have a pale yellow, soup-like consistency.

While the dal is cooking, fry the onion and garlic in the ghee until the onions are pale brown.

Add the turmeric and garam masala to the onions and cook for 2 or 3 seconds.

Stir the onion mixture into the cooked lentils. Serve hot, sprinkled with chopped tomato and green coriander.

SAG PANIR

Here, curd cheese cubes are combined with spicy spinach.

Serves 3–4

Preparation and cooking time: 40–45 minutes

2 pints (1.15 litres) whole milk
4 tablespoons lemon juice
Oil for deep frying
4 tablespoons vegetable oil
1 cup curry sauce (page 20)
16 oz (450g) can puréed spinach
½ teaspoon salt
1 teaspoon ground cummin
½ teaspoon chilli powder
1 teaspoon garam masala

Make the milk into curd cheese cubes as shown on page 94 for mattar panir.

Heat the 4 tablespoons of oil in a deep frying pan. When hot add the curry sauce and cook rapidly for about 5 minutes until quite thick.

Add the spinach and stir in the salt, ground cummin and chilli powder. Simmer, stirring, for 10 minutes.

Now add the cheese cubes and garam masala and continue to cook on a gentle heat for a further 5 minutes.

Serve.

MATTAR PANIR

This is a dish that is popular with vegetarians as it contains plenty of protein in the form of curd cheese cubes.

Serves 2–3.

Preparation and cooking time: 40–45 minutes

2 pints (1.15 litres) whole milk
4 tablespoons lemon juice
Oil for deep frying
6 oz (175g) frozen peas
4 tablespoons vegetable oil
½ pint (275ml or 2 cups) curry sauce (page 20)
1 level teaspoon salt
½ teaspoon turmeric
½ teaspoon ground coriander
½ teaspoon chilli powder
½ teaspoon garam masala
1 tablespoon single cream (optional)
2 teaspoons finely chopped green coriander

Bring the milk to the boil in a saucepan. Immediately add the lemon juice and stir until the milk appears to curdle. The solids should be visibly separated from the whey.

Strain through muslin or a clean tea towel. Place the curds, still in muslin, in a tray. Put something flat on it, such as a chopping board, and weight it down with something heavy. A large saucepan full of water is ideal. Leave for about 15 minutes. This squeezes all the liquid out of the curds.

When this is done, cut the flat slab of curds into approximately ½ inch (1cm) cubes, and deep fry in hot oil until golden on the outside. Drain.

Rinse the frozen peas in hot water and drain. Heat the oil in a deep frying pan and fry the peas in it for about 3 minutes.

Add the curry sauce and bring to a simmer. Stir in the salt, turmeric, ground coriander and chilli powder and simmer for 10 minutes.

Now add the cheese cubes and the garam masala. Simmer for a further 10 minutes.

Stir in the cream if used, and the green coriander.

Rice and Biryanis

MENU

PLAIN BOILED RICE

PILLAU RICE

PEAS PILLAU

FRIED RICE

CHICKEN BIRYANI

LAMB BIRYANI

PRAWN BIRYANI

VEGETABLE BIRYANI

COOKING RICE

My friends and customers are always telling me of their difficulty in cooking rice well. I must confess that this is one area where I once experienced considerable problems myself. Now that I can cook rice perfectly, I realise that my previous failures, and undoubtedly those of friends and customers, were due to inaccurate instructions which suggested using too much water. The rice invariably ends being soggy and mushy and the person cooking it thinks it is his or her fault. It clearly is not, as you will soon see.

For perfect results follow my recipes carefully and remember a few simple rules:

1. Always wash rice in several changes of water. This removes the starch left over from the milling process and helps to keep the grains separate during cooking.
2. Always drain the rice in a colander for about twenty

minutes until the grains are dry.

3. Use a heavy saucepan with a tight fitting lid, or cover the pan tightly with a sheet of aluminium foil before replacing lid.

4. Cook rice on a very low heat.

5. Always finish off in a preheated oven gas mark 3, 325°F (170°C) for about twenty minutes.

6. When stirring rice, always do so gently, using a fork to avoid breaking the grains.

Indian Restaurants use basmati rice, which, although more expensive than other varieties, has the right nutty aroma to complement our curries, in addition to being well suited for the sweet rice dishes popular in India.

PLAIN BOILED RICE

Quick and easy to prepare, this is the simplest of all the rice dishes.

Serves 4

Preparation and cooking time: 25–30 minutes

3 pints (1.7 litres) approx. water
2 cups basmati rice
1 teaspoon salt

Pour the water into a large pot and bring to the boil on a high heat.

Meanwhile pick over the rice and wash in several changes of water. Drain.

Add rice and salt to boiling water and bring back to the boil. Turn down the heat and stir.

Simmer the rice uncovered for 20 minutes, stirring occasionally.

In the meantime heat the oven to gas mark 3 (350°F or 170°C).

Drain into a large sieve, pour over cold water to remove excess starch and shake sieve to drain off as much water as possible.

Return rice to pot and place in the oven for about 10 minutes to dry the grains.

NB. If you are not serving the rice immediately, allow it to drain in the sieve until cool (do not place in oven) and refrigerate. Re-heat when required in a microwave oven or covered in a conventional one.

PILLAU RICE

This colourful rice dish with its wonderful aroma is probably the most popular way of serving rice in Indian Restaurants. It is a modification of the lavish pullaos made with lashings of ghee, opulently flavoured with saffron and generously garnished with almonds, sultanas and silver "vark" that are served in parts of Northern India on festive occasions.

The dish familiar nowadays uses less ghee and relies on food colourings rather than the expensive saffron for its array of colours.

Serves 4

Preparation and cooking time: 30 minutes approx.

¼ teaspoon yellow food colouring
¼ teaspoon red food colouring
2 cups basmati rice
1 tablespoon vegetable ghee
2 teaspoons finely chopped onion
6 green cardamoms
1 by 2 inch (5cm) stick cinnamon
4 cloves
2 bayleaves
3 cups cold water
½ teaspoon salt

Mix each food colouring with about a tablespoon of water, keeping the two colours separate, and set aside.

Pick over the rice carefully for any stones and wash

thoroughly in several changes of water. Leave to drain in a colander or large sieve.

Meanwhile heat the ghee in a heavy pot, and fry the onion until just translucent. Add the cardamoms, cinnamon, cloves, and bay leaves and cook for 1 minute.

Add the rice to the pot and mix well to coat all the grains with the ghee.

Pour in the water, add the salt, stir and bring to the boil. Once boiling turn the heat to very low and cover the pot with a tight fitting lid.

Switch on the oven to preheat to gas mark 3 (350°F or 170°C).

After 5 minutes stir rice gently with a fork or a wooden spoon. Cover again for a further 3 minutes.

After this time stir the rice again, but very carefully to avoid breaking the grains which will by now have become softer. The best way to do this is to slide the spoon down the side of the pot and gently lift the rice at the bottom to the top. Cover again, and repeat this procedure after a further 2 minutes. This method ensures that all the rice cooks evenly and you don't get a soggy mass at the bottom of the pot whilst the top layer remains under-cooked.

Now take one of the food colourings and make two lines of colour across the rice. Repeat with the other food colouring and make two lines down.

Replace the lid and place the pot in the oven for 15–20 minutes to finish cooking the rice and set the colours.

Remove the rice from the oven and transfer to a suitable container layer by layer to avoid breaking the rice. Fluff up gently with a fork to distribute the coloured grains equally.

Serve immediately or cool and refrigerate for up to 3 days.

When re-heating, the ideal way is to use a microwave oven. If using a conventional oven, remember to cover the rice to prevent it drying up.

PEAS PILLAU

The Restaurant method of making peas pillau is to warm up ready made pillau rice (recipe page 100) with some frozen peas that have been thawed out in a little hot oil. You may wish to do just this if you have some left over pillau rice. If not, follow the recipe below, which I feel is the better way to make this rice dish.

Serves 4

Preparation and cooking time: 30 minutes approx.

2 cups basmati rice
1 tablespoon vegetable ghee
1 small onion finely chopped
½ lb (225g) frozen peas
4 green cardamoms
2 bayleaves
1 by 2 inch (5cm) stick cinnamon
1 teaspoon whole cummin seeds
3 cups cold water
1 teaspoon salt

Pick over the rice and wash in several changes of water. Leave to drain in a colander or sieve.

Heat the ghee in a heavy pot and fry the onion until transparent.

Add all the remaining ingredients except rice, water and salt, and cook on a gentle heat for 6–7 minutes, stirring now and again.

Add the drained rice and mix well. Stir in the water and salt and bring to the boil.

Cover the pot with a tight fitting lid and turn down the heat to very low.

Preheat oven to gas mark 3 (350°F or 170°C).

After 5 minutes stir the rice. Replace lid for a further 3 minutes. Stir very carefully after this time by sliding the spoon down the side of the pot and gently pushing the rice at the bottom, towards the top.

Place the covered pot in the hot oven for about 15 minutes to dry off the rice.

Transfer to another container layer by layer and fluff up with a fork.

If not using immediately, cool, and keep covered in the refrigerator for up to 2 days.

NB. Peas Pillau made in this way is delicious eaten cold with spiced yoghurt (recipe page 113).

FRIED RICE

This is a tasty variation of a simple rice dish. Use half of the boiled rice from page 99 to create two different rice dishes in moments.

Serves 2

Preparation and cooking time: 5–10 minutes

2 tablespoons vegetable ghee
½ small onion finely chopped
1 cup basmati rice, boiled (page 99)

Heat the ghee in a pan and fry the onion until just beginning to brown.
Warm the rice and add to the pan. Toss around in the pan for a minute or two.
Serve immediately.

BIRYANIS

Consisting of layers of cooked rice and meat, traditionally biryanis are served on grand festive occasions when they are always made with generous helpings of ghee and perfumed with saffron. Nowadays, particularly in Restaurant cooking, vegetable ghee, oil and food colourings are substituted for these rather expensive ingredients.

A biryani is a meal in itself, although for those with a healthy appetite, a yoghurt dish or a vegetable side dish may make a good addition.

The recipes here are for meat or fish biryanis but vegetables may be substituted to make a vegetarian meal.

CHICKEN BIRYANI

Serves 4

Preparation and cooking time: 10 minutes approx.

1 lb (450g) cooked chicken (see page 49)
2 tablespoons vegetable oil
1 tablespoon cashew nuts roughly chopped
1 tablespoon sultanas
4 cups pillau rice
4 cups curry sauce
1 teaspoon garam masala
1 teaspoon chilli powder (or to taste)
½ teaspoon salt

Divide each chicken piece into two smaller pieces and set them aside.

Heat the oil in a pan. When hot, put the nuts into it and stir around until they turn light golden in colour. Remove with a slotted spoon and spread them out on a plate lined with kitchen paper.

Drop the sultanas into the same hot oil. They will plump up in a second or two. Remove immediately and put them on the same plate as the nuts.

Now put the chicken pieces into the pan and stir. Turn down the heat to very low.

Warm the rice for about 2 minutes in a microwave oven. Add to the chicken.

Stir very gently to avoid breaking the grains. Heat for 2 or 3 minutes tossing the rice and chicken rather than stirring.

Put the rice and chicken in a serving dish and keep warm.

Pour the curry sauce into a clean pan and bring to a simmer. Stir in the garam masala, chilli powder and salt.

Pour the sauce into serving dishes, spinkle the biryani with the nuts and sultanas and serve.

LAMB BIRYANI

Follow the recipe for Chicken Biryani on previous page, substituting the chicken with the same quantity of cooked lamb.

PRAWN BIRYANI

Follow the recipe for Chicken Biryani on previous page replacing the chicken with about 12 oz (350g) of prawns cooked in a little hot oil for 3 to 4 minutes.

VEGETABLE BIRYANI

Follow the recipe for Chicken Biryani but use about 12 oz (350g) diced cooked vegetables of your choice instead of the chicken.

12

Yogurts and Yogurt Drinks

MENU

CUCUMBER RAITA

RAITA WITH RADISH

SPICED YOGHURT

YOGHURT FLAVOURED WITH GARLIC AND CUMMIN

YOGHURT DRINKS

LASSI

YOGHURT

If your experience of yoghurt has been limited to the shop bought variety, then the taste of home-made yoghurt will surprise you. It is much less tart and so much more pleasant that even when eaten plain it is very palatable. Add a few spices and vegetables to it and it becomes delicious.

In India the goodness and versatility of yoghurt is exploited to the full. Its versatility is demonstrated by the wide variety of uses such as for sauces, marinades, as a lightener in breads, or as an accompaniment to meals sweetened or spiced. Nutritionally, yoghurt is rich in protein and is easier to digest than milk, having the necessary flora for a healthy digestion. It is little wonder then that Indian homes are seldom without it and that it is served at almost every meal.

Indian restaurants use yoghurt mainly as a marinade to tenderize meat and fish. Although it is offered as a side dish on the menu, few people ask for it. I believe this is because westerners are not familiar with yoghurt as part of a main meal, being more used to eating it sweetened and then only if health or diet conscious. This is a pity, and I would urge you to try some of my recipes as I am convinced you will like them.

Yoghurt is particularly good eaten with rice or parathas as a main meal, or as a cooling side dish with the more "dry" curries and bhajees.

HOW TO MAKE YOGHURT

To make yoghurt at home you will need some milk and a little live yoghurt. You may use full cream milk, semi-skimmed or skimmed milk, or even soya milk if you prefer. Full cream milk will obviously result in a creamier yoghurt which is nicer for eating but skimmed or semi-skimmed also produces a good result, particularly if you use my suggestion of adding a little skimmed milk powder to the warm milk.

The live yoghurt or "starter" that is added to warm milk requires continuing warmth to allow the culture in the starter to grow and turn the milk into yoghurt. I have never used a thermometer for this purpose, relying on my own perception, but should you need to do so, a temperature between 30°C–38°C (85°F–100°F) is ideal. Much warmer than this and the milk will curdle. Much cooler and it will not set.

After adding the starter to the milk, it needs to be kept warm for a few hours to allow the culture to do its work. In the Restaurant we would place the pot on top of the tandoor once it has been closed down, with the glowing embers still keeping the tandoor warm, and wrap the pot in several teatowels to hold in the heat. At home a warm airing cupboard is just as suitable.

If you find you really have a taste for home-made yoghurt, it is worth investing in a yoghurt maker. I use one at home and find this to be the easiest and most convenient way of making yoghurt.

You will require:

1 pint (570ml) milk
1 tablespoon live plain yoghurt
2 tablespoons skimmed milk powder (optional)

Bring the milk to the boil in a saucepan. Cover and leave to cool until warm to the touch. If using a thermometer around 40°C (105°F) is ideal.

Beat the yoghurt with a spoon until smooth and mix it into the milk, stirring in the skin that will have formed on top of the milk. Also stir in the skimmed milk powder if using.

Warm a bowl or any suitable non-metallic container and pour in the milk. Cover and wrap with towels or an old shawl.

Set aside in a warm place as suggested for around 4–6 hours.

Refrigerate the yoghurt until required. It will keep in perfect condition for up to 5 days.

TIP: Removing the yoghurt from the warmth as quickly as possible after it has set will result in a sweeter yoghurt ideal for eating. If you are planning to use the yoghurt for marinating purposes only, leave it an hour or two after it has set to make it more tart.

CUCUMBER RAITA

This is a delicious, cooling yoghurt dish excellent served with spicy curries together with rice and/or Indian breads.

Serves 4

Preparation time: 5 minutes

1 pint (570ml) plain yoghurt
1 teaspoon salt
4 inch (10cm) piece of cucumber
½ teaspoon garam masala
Freshly ground black pepper

Put the yoghurt and salt into a bowl and beat with a fork until smooth.

Thinly slice cucumber, place slices on top of each other and cut into strips. Now cut the strips into dice. Scatter over yoghurt.

Cover and refrigerate until required. Sprinkle on the garam masala and black pepper just before serving.

NB. Allow the yoghurt to reach room temperature before serving.

RAITA WITH RADISH

This raita has more bite than cucumber raita and is delicious eaten on its own as well as with rice and curries. The radish used in this recipe is known as **mooli**. This is white in colour and shaped rather like a large carrot. It is sweeter in taste than the well known smaller red radishes and is excellent in salads. Moolis are now readily available in supermarkets as well as Asian greengrocers. If you cannot get them, use whatever radish you can easily find.

Serves 4

Preparation time: 5 minutes

1 pint (570ml) plain yoghurt
1 teaspoon salt
5 inch (13cm) piece mooli
½ teaspoon garam masala
1 green chilli finely chopped

Put the yoghurt and salt into a bowl and beat with a fork until smooth.

Peel, wash and grate the mooli. Add to the yoghurt together with the garam masala and the chilli.

Mix and refrigerate until required.

SPICED YOGHURT

This is a simple yoghurt dish that can be served with any meal.

Serves 4

Preparation time: 2–3 minutes

1 pint (570ml) plain yoghurt
4 tablespoons milk
1 teaspoon salt
½ teaspoon garam masala
½ teaspoon chilli powder

Put all ingredients into a bowl and mix thoroughly. Cover and refrigerate until ready to serve.

YOGHURT FLAVOURED WITH GARLIC AND CUMMIN

The combination of garlic and cummin flavours is quite unusual in a yoghurt dish, but the wonderful taste of this preparation only serves to illustrate the wide variety of ingredients that can be successfully added to yoghurt.

Serves 4

Preparation time: 4–5 minutes

1 pint (570ml) plain yoghurt
1 teaspoon salt
1 small clove garlic
½–1 green chilli finely chopped
1 teaspoon whole cummin
2 teaspoons finely chopped onion
Pinch turmeric

Put the yoghurt and salt into a bowl and beat with a fork until smooth and creamy.

Crush the garlic using a garlic press or chop very finely.

Add to yoghurt together with the remaining ingredients and mix.

Serve immediately or keep in the refrigerator until required.

YOGHURT DRINKS

Even now in modern India, many people keep livestock for milk. Milking takes place very early each morning. Towards the end of the day, the milk that remains after the day's requirements is boiled, cooled and poured into large clay urns which are left overnight to produce yoghurt for the following day. The important task of churning the yoghurt to make butter (makhan) is undertaken with great enthusiasm at the crack of dawn. Some of the makhan is eaten as it is with yoghurt and breads and the rest is heated and clarified to make ghee. The liquid that is left after churning the yoghurt and removing the makhan is the lassi.

Lassi is a refreshing and nutritious drink that is served throughout the heat of the day and also with meals instead of water.

I do not expect you to go through this lengthy process in order to enjoy home made lassi, so you will find the following method quick, simple and perfectly acceptable.

LASSI (Sweet or Sour)

Makes almost 1 pint (570ml)

Preparation time: 2–3 minutes

½ pint (275ml) plain yoghurt
½ pint (275ml) cold water
½ teaspoon salt
Freshly ground black pepper (optional) } *for sour lassi*
2 teaspoons sugar *for sweet lassi*

Place all ingredients in a bowl and whisk until frothy. Serve in tall glasses with plenty of ice.

13

Sweets

MENU

KULFI

GULAB JAMONS

MANGOES

TROPICAL FRUIT SALAD

KULFI

Kulfi is sometimes known as Indian Ice-cream. I have tried many varieties of Kulfi throughout the country; this recipe produces by far the best I have ever eaten. It serves 8.

Preparation and cooking time: 1hr 30 minutes approx.

4 pints (2¼ litres) whole milk
12 green cardamoms
10 tablespoons granulated sugar
3 tablespoons flaked almonds
½ pint (275ml) single cream
2 tablespoons finely chopped unsalted pistachios

Bring the milk to a boil in a heavy pot. Turn down the heat so as to allow the milk to simmer vigorously without boiling over.

The milk must reduce considerably, to about one third of its original amount. Stir frequently as the milk simmers, incorporating the skin that forms on the top, and scrape and stir in the milk that dries and sticks to the sides of the pot.

While the milk is simmering, take the seeds out of the cardamom pods and grind finely. Stir them into the milk.

When the milk has reduced sufficiently, stir in the sugar and almonds. Simmer for 2–3 minutes until the sugar dissolves completely.

Take the milk off the heat and allow it to cool slightly. Stir in the cream and half the pistachios.

Pour into a square or rectangular vessel that will allow the mixture to sit 2–3 inches (5–7.5cm) deep. Cool completely. Cover and place in the freezer for about 30 minutes. Sprinkle over the remaining pistachios and return to freezer until set. Remove the Kulfi from the freezer 15 minutes before serving and cut it into ½ inch (1cm) cubes.

GULAB JAMONS

These are very light, soft, sponge-like sweets soaked in a light, flavoured syrup. They are easy to make and a delicious conclusion to a spicy meal. Serve warm or cold.

Allow three to four per person and sprinkle with a little brandy for a really special sweet.

Makes 16

Preparation and cooking time: 30 minutes approx.

For syrup:

8 oz (225g) granulated sugar
6 green cardamoms
4 cups water

For jamons:

6 tablespoons full fat milk powder
2 tablespoons Self-Raising flour
1 tablespoon melted butter
A little cold milk to bind
Oil for deep frying

Put the sugar, cardamoms and water into a pot and bring to the boil. Turn down the heat and simmer the syrup for about 15 minutes.

Meanwhile sift the milk powder and flour into a bowl.

Add the melted butter and rub into mixture with fingertips until it resembles fine breadcrumbs.

Add the milk a little at a time, drawing in the mixture to form a soft dough.

Put the oil on to heat and divide the dough into 16 parts. Roll each one out in the palms of your hands into a little ball.

The syrup should be ready by now. Take it off the heat so that it may cool slightly before having the jamons put into it.

Test the oil by putting in one ball of dough. The oil must only just be hot enough to make the dough rise to the surface after a few seconds and to fry it very gently. Adjust as necessary.

When the oil is at the right heat, put in as many balls of dough as your pan or karahi will easily take.

Move the pan about carefully to keep the jamons moving until they rise to the surface of the oil.

When they are at the surface keep moving them about with a slotted spoon to ensure that they cook evenly.

The jamons will almost double in size as they are cooking and will turn a deep, golden brown colour. This should take about 4–5 minutes.

Drain on kitchen paper, allow to cool for 5 minutes and drop them into the syrup.

The jamons will be very soft and easily broken until they have cooled, when the texture will become firmer.

Serve with a few tablespoons of the syrup for each person.

MANGOES

Fresh mangoes are amongst the finest fruits in the world. Soft, sweet, ripe mangoes make an excellent dessert, fit for any occasion.

When buying fresh mangoes, look for those with a strong mango aroma, and a clear yellow skin with reddish patches. Ripe fruits should also yield slightly when squeezed. A mango has a large stone. To serve, cut this out and either peel and cut into slices or, and this is the method used in most restaurants, cut the fruit in half along its length leaving the skin on. Cut out the stone, and turn the fruit inside out revealing the flesh uppermost. Make slits in the flesh, right down to the skin, lengthwise about ½ inch (1cm) apart and then crosswise to create a "hedgehog".

TROPICAL FRUIT SALAD

Served chilled this is an exotic and refreshing sweet, ideal after a spicy meal.

We always use canned fruits for this as they are very good but you may like to try it with fresh fruits as they are readily available from most supermarkets.

Serves 6–8

1 can sliced mangoes
1 can guavas
1 can lychees

Drain about half of the syrup out of each can and combine all the fruit in a salad bowl.

Chill for at least half an hour before serving.

INDEX

CHINESE COOKERY SECRETS
How to Cook Chinese Restaurant Food at Home

Deh-Ta Hsiung shares his life-long knowledge of Chinese *restaurant* cooking to help you successfully reproduce your favourite meals at home – from a simple, single dish to an elaborate grand feast. He shows you each crucial stage of preparation to enable you to recreate the harmonious blending of subtle flavours, delicate textures, aromas, colours and shapes that are the hallmarks of authentic Chinese restaurant cooking.

THE FAN OVEN BOOK

Cooking in a fan oven is *different*. Jenny Webb will help you to understand how your fan oven works, and how to get the best from it. She includes a simple-to-use conversion chart so you can easily convert the temperatures or settings used in your former conventional oven to the new ones you'll need now. Her book is packed with recipes.

AN INDIAN HOUSEWIFE'S RECIPE BOOK

A collection of over 100 traditional Indian recipes handed down to Laxmi Khurana through the generations and admired by her family and friends. Not only are curries featured – meat, vegetable and dhal – but there is an array of starters, raitas, chutneys, pickles and sweets. Everything, in fact, that characterises Indian cookery for people all over the world.

SUPER SOUPS & SAUCES

Annette Yates provides a real feast of real soups for every season and reason: light and chilled for a warm summer's day; smooth, puréed or creamed for that formal occasion; hearty and thick – a meal in itself – for a cold winter evening. Discover, too, an array of ideas for attractive, tasty garnishes. Plus subtle, rich, savoury, sweet, traditional or quick-to-make sauces to transform everyday meals or turn that special party dish into a true culinary delight.

FRESH BREAD IN THE MORNING

Wake up to the aroma of fresh bread wafting through your kitchen every morning! A dream? No. With your bread machine it's a reality. Annette Yates has set about reducing ingredients such as yeast, salt, sugar, fat and dried milk powder, providing recipes for making loaves that are natural and delicious.

ICE 'N' EASY

Here, favourite cookery writer, Annette Yates, shows how to make luscious creamy concoctions, light-and-airy yoghurt mixtures and dairy-free ice creams, as well as sorbets, granitas and slushy drinks.

MICROWAVE COOKING PROPERLY EXPLAINED

Annette Yates explains simply and clearly how a microwave cooker works, and helps you choose the best equipment. Planned from first principles for both the present and prospective microwave owner, the book shows how the versatile microwave cooker can transform life for the busy cook.

THE MICROWAVE PLANNER

Find out how to *adapt* your favourite recipes to microwave cooking and how to *plan* so as to maximise the benefits of the microwave cooker. The book is designed for fast reference and jam-packed with practical advice to help you fit the microwave naturally into your own system of cooking.

MICROWAVE RECIPES FOR ONE

This book is written specifically for the person who lives alone or who has to prepare individual meals for another reason. It contains an indispensable cooking guide which explains how to adapt family recipe instructions to the smaller amounts needed for a single portion.

MICROWAVE COOKING TIMES AT A GLANCE!

An essential book for anyone with a microwave. With the contents in alphabetical order and each food item presented in tabular form it's easy to find the information you need and it can be seen clearly *at a glance*! Tips and hints about preparing and cooking different sorts of food are also included. What's more, the tables cover all powers of microwave up to 1000W, so there's no need to do fiddly calculations to convert cooking times for your own oven.

RIGHT WAY
PUBLISHING POLICY

HOW WE SELECT TITLES

RIGHT WAY consider carefully every deserving manuscript. Where an author is an authority on his subject but an inexperienced writer, we provide first-class editorial help. The standards we set make sure that every **RIGHT WAY** book is practical, easy to understand, concise, informative and delightful to read. Our specialist artists are skilled at creating simple illustrations which augment the text wherever necessary.

CONSISTENT QUALITY

At every reprint our books are updated where appropriate, giving our authors the opportunity to include new information.

FAST DELIVERY

We sell **RIGHT WAY** books to the best bookshops throughout the world. It may be that your bookseller has run out of stock of a particular title. If so, he can order more from us at any time – we have a fine reputation for "same day" despatch, and we supply any order, however small (even a single copy), to any bookseller who has an account with us. We prefer you to buy from your bookseller, as this reminds him of the strong underlying public demand for **RIGHT WAY** books. However, you can order direct from us by post or by phone with a credit card.

FREE

If you would like an up-to-date list of all **RIGHT WAY** titles currently available, please send a stamped self-addressed envelope to ELLIOT RIGHT WAY BOOKS, BRIGHTON ROAD, LOWER KINGSWOOD, TADWORTH, SURREY, KT20 6TD, U.K. or visit our website at www.right-way.co.uk